Answering Skeptics

Answering Skeptics

SHARING YOUR FAITH
WITH CRITICS, DOUBTERS,
AND SEEKERS

DOUGLAS JACOBY

NASHVILLE

NEW YORK • LONDON • MELBOURNE • VANCOUVER

Answering Skeptics

SHARING YOUR FAITH WITH CRITICS, DOUBTERS, AND SEEKERS

© 2017 DOUGLAS JACOBY

Published in New York, New York, by Morgan James Publishing. Morgan James and The Entrepreneurial Publisher are trademarks of Morgan James, LLC.
www.MorganJamesPublishing.com

The Morgan James Speakers Group can bring authors to your live event. For more information or to book an event visit The Morgan James Speakers Group at
www.TheMorganJamesSpeakersGroup.com.

ISBN 978-1-68350-028-5 paperback
ISBN 978-1-68350-030-8 eBook
ISBN 978-1-68350-029-2 hardcover
Library of Congress Control Number: 2016906019

Cover Design by:
Chris Treccani
www.3dogdesign.net

Interior Design by:
Bonnie Bushman
The Whole Caboodle Graphic Design

In an effort to support local communities, raise awareness and funds, Morgan James Publishing donates a percentage of all book sales for the life of each book to Habitat for Humanity Peninsula and Greater Williamsburg.

Get involved today! Visit
www.MorganJamesBuilds.com

Dedication

To our church family at North River.

Table of Contents

Acknowledgments

I owe a debt of gratitude to the trio of Elizabeth, Terry, Tiffany. Like a baby, the book grew inside me – and you delivered it.

Introduction

I wasn't brought up in a Bible-centered household—perhaps this was your own situation. Although six copies of the Holy Bible stood in our bookshelf, not once in my childhood did I see another family member reading Scripture. In fact, I don't think I ever saw *anyone* reading the Bible, even in church.

Our parents drove us to church most Sundays, but aside from a perfunctory table grace ("God is great, God is good, let us thank him for our food, amen"), we didn't talk about faith at the dinner table or at any other time. I never heard my parents pray. So it is no surprise that I absorbed the view, especially during secondary school, that although Christianity had had an enormous impact on culture, it was now out of fashion. I wondered what had happened to Christianity. And why was Christ so controversial?

At age sixteen I met a Bible believer—the first in my life—and he connected me with other believers. Most of them were timid in terms of outreach—they rarely shared their faith, though they considered themselves good Christians. I had mixed feelings. I admired Christ, but I didn't particularly admire his followers. I believed in God, was intrigued by faith, and deep down longed for something authentic. But if I was going to accept Christianity, it had to be true, and it had to be defensible. My circle of friends—most were Jewish or agnostic—were thinkers who didn't hesitate to express their own ideas, or to shoot down yours if they disagreed. If I was going to be a Christian, I would need to be prepared.

The safest course seemed to read up on the faith to which I was slowly being drawn. Better said, it was *Christ* to whom I was being drawn (John 12:32). The more I read, mainly evidences books with titles like *Know Why You Believe,* the more excitement I felt. The more I read, the more I thought through the issues, the more convinced I became. My faith was strengthening, but I seldom spoke of it to anyone.

By the time I went off to college, I was ready for a change. Living away from home, I could have a fresh start! The Lord heard the unspoken prayer of my heart, and on my second day at Duke University, there came a knock at my door, inviting me to a Bible study group. Accepting the invitation put me on the fast track to discipleship, though I did not yet realize it. One thing led to another, and a few weeks later I surrendered to Christ in the water of baptism.

So there I was, a young man on fire for God, by his providence studying in an elite and very secular university. When I made claims about faith in class or in conversation, few people took my word for it. That was good for me. I couldn't be sloppy; I had to know my stuff, or in biblical lingo, "be prepared to answer" (1 Pet 3:15).

I have now been wrestling with faith issues for forty years, trying to answer others' questions (and my own). Since my university days, I've spent many years living in large cities, where I've been exposed to a wide variety of cultures and faiths. My wife and I have resided in multiple countries, and I've been privileged to teach in most of the world's nations. This has forced me to wrestle with how to relate to agnostics, Muslims, Buddhists, Hindus, atheists, doubters, and others. One of my current jobs is teaching in a MA program in Bible and Theology at Lincoln Christian University, teaching two classes: Apologetics and World Religions (emphasis on Islam).

In *Answering Skeptics,* we're going to explore the field of Christian evidences, with the goal of equipping you to answer most questions you might encounter. The Bible urges us,

Always be prepared to give an answer to everyone who asks you to give a reason for the hope you have. But do this with gentleness and respect, keeping a clear conscience, so that those who speak maliciously about your good behavior in Christ may be ashamed of their slander. (1 Pet 3:15–16)

Every suggestion in *Answering Skeptics* comes from actual conversations in my own evangelism. This book is a compilation of the hundreds of questions I've fielded in conversations, classrooms, and churches around the world, and the responses I've found most effective. In each chapter we'll consider practical responses to common challenges from skeptics, atheists, and other critics of faith.

Playing offense vs. playing defense

Christian evidences has two sides, one offensive and one defensive. The offensive side involves the presentation of reasons for faith. The defensive side deals mainly with objections (for example, "contradictions" in the Bible). In this book we'll be playing a bit of both. You'll equip yourself to explain your faith in reasonable terms (offense); and also learn how to counter false objections to faith in general and to Christianity specifically (defense). You'll find answers to most basic questions you'll encounter when befriending or engaging a skeptic.

Rules of engagement

When discussing questions of faith, remember these principles:

1. **Listen first and listen well (James 1:19).** Ask questions. Draw out your friend's thoughts. Get to know their religious history—why they feel the way they do, where their ideas and information come from, how thoroughly they have studied the topics at hand. Make sure you understand what your friend's questions and objections to faith actually are, rather than making assumptions.

2. **When you don't know the answer to a question, don't make something up.** Say, "I don't have an answer for that right now,

but let me look into it and get back to you." And realize (as you will see in the book) that not all questions have "perfect answers"—and yet God always gives us enough to make an informed decision.

3. **Speak with confidence and courage, but not cockiness.** Be respectful of your friend's perspective and questions (Col 4:6; Acts 26:1–3, 25–27).

4. **Don't let vigorous discussion descend into heated argument.** It's fine to disagree—even to disagree passionately—but there's no need to throw insults or accusations. Know when it's time to take a break or end a discussion altogether.

5. **Pray.** Pray for wisdom, and for God to open the doors of your friend's heart (Acts 16:14).

Christian living is the best evidence

Keep in mind that your life may be the best "proof" of Christianity that you can offer to your skeptical friends. When they see compassion, courage, humility, honesty, and forgiveness in your life, those qualities are a powerful testimony to the hand of God at work in the real world.

Also notice that I have repeatedly used the word *friend*. I urge you to be a friend to unbelievers. Get to know them. Invite them into your home and into your heart.

Once you have addressed your friend's questions, encourage them to read the Bible for themselves and even try putting Christian principles into practice. Urge them to give the Bible a try—to see if the principles help them grow, and make their relationships better. As Jesus himself promised, "Anyone who chooses to do the will of God will find out whether my teaching comes from God or whether I speak on my own" (John 7:17).

How to use this book

Answering Skeptics covers eight broad areas: Roadblocks to Faith; Scripture; Morality; God; Science; Suffering; Jesus and Miracles; and World Religions. Our approach is going to be simple: in most chapters, I present the skeptic's questions and objections on the topic, and some responses you may offer them. The responses are not exhaustive, but they are sufficient to allow for a knowledgeable and productive discussion. The goal of this book: to offer basic responses that you will be able to try out immediately.

I pray you find *Answering Skeptics* a useful and practical tool, and that it helps you bring new friends to faith in our God.

Part 1:
ROADBLOCKS TO FAITH

1. Hypocrisy in Christianity
2. Don't Judge Me!
3. Intolerance

Sometimes a conversation stops before it even gets started—and this is especially true when discussing matters of faith. If you want to engage a skeptical friend in a meaningful discussion about faith, God, or the Bible, you may first have to get past some roadblocks.

Some people have been so turned off by hypocrisy in Christianity that they won't even consider it. Chapter 1, Hypocrisy in Christianity, offers responses that may help people to work through their concerns and give faith an honest look.

Others have a different issue: defensiveness. The minute a conversation about religion becomes too personal, they put up the defense, "Don't judge me!" This keeps our conversations at a shallow level. If we are ever to introduce people to the real principles of following Christ, we have to find a way past this shield.

And lastly, there is the thorny issue of intolerance. Our modern world places great value on inclusiveness and acceptance, and has redefined tolerance in a way that sometimes makes it difficult to share our faith. How do we explain Christianity to a modern thinker, and help them understand the difference between respectful disagreement and unkind intolerance?

CHAPTER 1

Hypocrisy in Christianity

*M*any people who count themselves skeptics have been turned off to God and the Bible not by intellectual objections, but by personal ones. We've heard the charge so many times: "Christianity has so many hypocrites!"

When we take a close look at the church, sadly, the statement rings true. Recent polls suggest that even in the religious United States only seventeen percent of Christians are serious enough about their faith to attend church every Sunday, and other polls turn up a deplorable level of Bible knowledge.[1] Christian families are not immune to divorce,[2] while surveys reveal the majority of Christian men indulge in pornography.[3]

The critics' point may be valid, yet it's hardly original. Unbelievers are usually unaware of this, but the Scriptures challenge hypocrisy with white-hot intensity. Jesus lambastes the hypocrites (Matt 7:1, 23:1–36). Paul echoes the accusation, reminding his readers, "The name of God is blasphemed among the Gentiles because of you" (Rom 2:1–24; Isa 52:5). This is a point the Bible takes with devastating seriousness.

Here we must make an important logical point. Critics routinely confuse the messenger with the message. A salesman might be a poor representative for an otherwise great product. Perhaps he's selling memberships to a health club, but he is lethargic or obese. There's no direct connection between his physical condition and the health club—though no one doubts he could be turning off prospective members. He may simply be in the wrong line of work. Or a physician might abuse his authority, or prescribe the wrong medication. Would we be rational to reject all of medicine just because of a bad experience or two? Of course not. A messenger may discredit the message, but that's not the same as disproving it.

Let's steer our friends towards the message, reminding them that instances of failed faith are no excuse for ignoring God. At the same time, we enhance the credibility of the gospel by living it out in our own lives.

It should be noted that in the case of some skeptics, their objection is sincere. They have been deeply wounded by church or religion. For others, the claim is just an excuse. We should aim for sensitivity, so that we may discern which is the case.

Finally, when someone says, "No thanks, I'll pass on your invitation to church—too many hypocrites," maybe we can quip, "There's always room for one more." After all, hypocrisy isn't the special province of the religious. It's everywhere! Hypocrisy may even be lower among believers, given that the Lord took such a strong stand against going through the motions. So let's not just roll over when the skeptic claims the high ground.

In short, there's no perfect group, and the church is no exception. And even if there were a perfect church, the day you or I joined, it would cease being perfect.

Points to Remember:

When someone objects to organized religion because of its hypocrisy, here are ways we can respond:

- "You're right. Sadly, there are a lot of hypocrites. The Bible agrees with your criticism, and assures us that the Lord will deal severely with them." This response is affirming and disarming.

- Let's not confuse the messenger with the message. Someone may be a poor representative of a good product. We must distinguish between the two. A poor representative of Christianity hardly disproves the teachings of Christ. Insist on this: hypocrisy may discredit, but it does not disprove.
- No one has cornered the market on hypocrisy. (And the one without sin should cast the first stone.) Encourage your friend to acknowledge that hypocrites are everywhere—not just in Christianity. Everyone has weaknesses to grow in.

CHAPTER 2

Don't Judge Me!

*J*t has been said that the most quoted Bible verse is no longer John 3:16. Now it's Matthew 7:1: "Judge not." Those two words are often used as a shield, blocking any discussion that might hit too close to home. Quite often, when someone pleads, "Judge not!", he's just being defensive. The moment a conversation about faith becomes too personal, requiring honest self-reflection or a willingness to admit error or make a change, the person throws up the shield: "Judge not!"

Biblical definitions of judging

I put this study together when we lived in Sweden, some twenty-five years ago. In any culture—whether liberal Sweden of 1990 or liberal America of 2017—thinking biblically demands that we come to terms with what the Scriptures say about this important subject. Certainly, a judgmental spirit is unbiblical and unbecoming of a believer, but just because some people judge wrongly, not all judging is wrong. In fact, the Bible distinguishes a number of types of judging—some good, some bad. Let's take a look at all the different types of judgment.

1. Hypocritical judging (Matt 7:1–5; Rom 2:1)
This is the kind of judging most people have in mind when they express the judgment that one shouldn't judge. Jesus tells us to get the log out of our own eye so that we can see clearly enough to help our brother. Clearly he expects us to do a certain amount of "judging"—but not hypocritically.

2. Discerning those receptive to the gospel (Matt 7:6, 10:11–16)
It is not unkind to judge who is open to the gospel message and who isn't. It's what is fairest to all—both to the person at hand as well as to others who may be seeking the Lord (7:7).

3. Superficial judging (John 7:24)
We are called to get the facts and know the Scriptures. That is the only way to make a "right judgment" in basic matters of daily life: What's right or wrong? What's best? What pleases God? What's wise and what's foolish? The entire book of Proverbs exhorts us to this sort of practical wisdom. The person who fails to make a right judgment will make poor decisions, and may even be duped by others more shrewd.

4. Making an assessment (Acts 4:19)
The act of judgment itself is neutral. The usual Greek verb for judge or discern is *krinein*. It is not an inherently negative word. It means moving from premises to conclusions; assessing a situation; discerning. As we will urge in the next chapter, we ought to think clearly when assessing the claims of the various world religions; this kind of evaluation is not inherently ungracious. In fact, Paul insists that the spiritual man makes all sorts of judgments (1 Cor 2:15). That kind of judgment is good.

5. Passing judgment on opinion matters (Rom 14:1)
We must all take a stand on the crucial issues, but it is wrong to judge others on the basis of peripheral matters or non-salvation issues. (In Rom 14, the disputable matter concerns foods.) Of course the apostles expect us to accept the weaker brother, not necessarily to leave him in a state of ignorance or weak faith. Yet the Lord will hold all of us accountable for

how we use our freedom of thought and expression, and there are many passages in the Bible reminding us of this truth.

6. Final judgment (Rom 14:10–12; Acts 10:42)
Final judgment is God's prerogative, and his alone. Sentencing people to heaven or hell is "final judgment." Obviously, no human has the authority to send any other human being anywhere after death. Further, do not confuse judging in the sense of *warning* with judging in the sense of *sentencing*; they are different things.

7. Judging hearts and motives (1 Cor 4:3–5)
This type of judging is highly problematic, and so the Bible discourages it. Yes, out of the mouth comes the overflow of the heart (Luke 6:45), so we may have some clues to what is going on in someone's heart or mind, and yet Proverbs says that only a person of understanding can draw out the innermost intent (20:5). Paul adds that he does not even judge himself. Let's not get tied in knots trying to analyze everybody—including ourselves!

8. Disciplinary judging (1 Cor 5:12–13)
Church discipline requires that action be taken when serious sin is affecting the congregation. This may include expelling the unrepentant.

9. Judging disputes (1 Cor 6:1–6)
Judging disputes requires judgment (discernment). The apostle assumes that Christians have the collective wisdom to settle their own conflicts without going public.

10. Critical judging (Jas 4:11–12)
Grumbling—for example, rich Christians complaining against poor Christians, or vice versa—is wrong. We are not to judge others in a critical, destructive manner (Eph 4:29). Before I correct someone else, I need to examine my heart (as far as that is possible), to know whether I am trying to guide, help, or educate in love, or whether my intention comes from an arrogant desire to defeat, tear down, and humiliate.

11. Interpreting the Scriptures (1 Cor 10:15, 11:13)
We are all encouraged to correctly study and interpret God's word. This entails exercising judgment.

12. Doctrinal nit-picking (Col 2:16)
The Bible discourages this type of judgment. Some believers insist that others are condemned by God on the basis of inconsequential or outmoded doctrines—in Col 2:16, Paul mentions observance of the Sabbath and rules about kosher foods. The central teachings of Scripture indicate which core doctrines play a role in salvation, and reveal that not all biblical teachings are equally important, or essential for salvation. This is not to say that we should refuse to "draw the line" when it comes to such key doctrines as the one body, spirit, hope, Lord, faith, baptism, and God (Eph 4:3–6). The Bible is too long, the lost are too many, and life is too short, for us to get bogged down in non-issues.

What kind of judgment does the Bible approve?
John 3:16 was too short a snippet to lead most people to repentance, granted. But at least it said *something*. Matthew 7:1, in the hands of most who wield it nowadays, says nothing at all. It may actually indicate a closed-minded attitude toward religion, a refusal even to consider or discuss. A person may insist, "Accept me! Don't judge me! I believe in tolerance!" But keep in mind that their "tolerance" may just be apathy in disguise. Or as someone put it, "The fellow who boasts about his open mind may only have a vacant one."

How should we respond when someone (often a non-believer) corrects us and tells us not to judge? Here are some suggestions: Ask them, "Do you know what Jesus was teaching by saying that?" They may not know. You can then explain, "Jesus did not want us to be hypocrites. He wanted us to look at our own life and clean it up in order to be able to help others compassionately." Then ask, "Are you aware that Jesus used that very statement to teach us how to render a clear judgment and to help others change best?" This will most likely be a new insight for them, and should take the discussion to a more productive level.

In our modern era, taking a stand for anything (conclusively) is considered ungracious. Yet we have seen that the common plea, "Judge not" is a gross oversimplification. We all must make many judgments every day. When we do, let's be sure we are doing it in the right spirit, about the right things.

"Judge not!" is often a simplistic (and evasive) move to escape responsibility or truth. But Christians are called to judge wisely, beginning with ourselves: "Examine yourselves to see whether you are in the faith; test yourselves. Do you not realize that Christ Jesus is in you—unless, of course, you fail the test?" (2 Cor 13:5).

Points to Remember:

- Forbidden forms of judgment include hypocritical judging, superficial judging, condemning in opinion matters, final judgment, judging motives, critical judging, and doctrinal nit-picking.
- Acceptable forms of judgment include discerning who is receptive to the gospel, making a "right" judgment, making a general assessment, disciplinary judgment, judging disputes, and interpreting the Scriptures correctly.

CHAPTER 3

Intolerance

*L*et us explore—and expel—a modern notion that muddies the waters of honest inquiry, and tilts the playing field decidedly against believers in God.

Many in our society find it hard to understand how a "loving God" would hold a "religious difference" against anyone. After all, aren't we all worshiping the same God? In fact, a survey of thirty-five thousand American adults shows that seventy percent believe there are many paths to God, all equally valid. Says Michael Lindsay of Rice University, "The survey shows religion in America is, indeed, three thousand miles wide and only three inches deep."[4] The problem is that people do not know why they believe what they believe, and certainly do not understand the uniqueness of the Christian system. Subscribing to such beliefs, they dismiss Jesus' exclusive claim, "I am the way and the truth and the life. No one comes to the Father except through me" (John 14:6). And with this kind of thinking so prevalent, religious persons are often accused of being judgmental, intolerant, and exclusivist.

The changing definition of tolerance

The word *tolerance* has undergone a substantial shift in meaning in recent decades, from acceptance of *persons* to acceptance of *ideas*. Christians ought to point out this change and challenge it; otherwise the common charge of bigotry may be difficult to shake. After all, we *accept* everybody, even if we don't agree with them. Besides, no one is tolerant of all ideas. Many critics of Christianity are highly intolerant of Christians.

We must help skeptics to understand that Christianity is inclusive, not exclusive. Of course, by its very nature, all truth *excludes* error (truth and untruth cannot both be right). Yet Christ's followers are actually inclusive—despite the negative message often conveyed in the media, and even in some of the seminary classes I have attended. In the spirit of 1 Tim 2:4, we truly desire everyone to be saved, regardless of their background. In Christ, barriers are broken down, and the church itself (the body of Christ) is a powerful visual aid: people see that everyone is welcome, as the demographic prejudices of society melt away. Here are some examples of tolerance drawn from Jesus' ministry and from the Bible:

- Jesus' own group of disciples provide an amazing model of tolerance. The twelve he chose as his apostles were drawn from groups who would naturally repel each other: the working class and the upper class, the politically neutral and the politically radical, Roman collaborators and the resistance. In spite of their differences, their connection to Christ taught them how to be unified.
- The Bible repeatedly urges us to respect others. If Christians follow their Lord's example, they will speak with respect— and more than respect, *love*—towards all people, including their enemies.
- Church is a great place to bring people together, despite their cultural, racial, and class differences. Jesus' plan of the communion meal ensured that all would come to the table as equals.

- Church is a place of reconciliation. Jesus expected his followers to join together in working through their differences, not suffer silently at home. Bitterness has no place, and in fact the Bible warns us that bitter refusal to reconcile will prevent us from seeing the Lord (Matt 18:21–35).

In his inaugural address as president of Fuller Theological Seminary (1955), Edward John Carnell called us to *humble* discernment:

Whoever meditates on the mystery of his own life will quickly realize why only God, the searcher of the secrets of the heart, can pass final judgment. We cannot judge what we have no access to. The self is a swirling conflict of fears, impulses, sentiments, interests, allergies, and foibles. It is a metaphysical given for which there is no easy rational explanation. Now if we cannot unveil the mystery of our own motives and affections, how much less can we unveil the mystery in others? That is, as we look into ourselves, we encounter the mystery of our own, the depths of our own selfhood. As we sing things like "Just as I am, though tossed about with many a conflict, many a doubt, fightings within and fears without, O Lamb of God, I come." And having recognized the mysteries that dwell in the very depths of our own being, how can we treat other people as if they were empty or superficial beings, without the same kind of mystery?

With these important considerations in mind, let's become all things to all men (1 Cor 9:22). This means we need to aim to understand how others think and feel, including members of other religions. If we don't make an effort to understand world religions, how will the grand vision of Revelation 7:9 ever become a reality?

After this I looked and there before me was a great multitude that no one could count, from every nation, tribe, people and language, standing before the throne and in front of the Lamb.

Points to Remember:

- We must be careful how we define tolerance. Remind the skeptic that Christians *accept* everybody, even if we don't agree with them. That does not make us intolerant.
- Christians can model inclusiveness by embracing friendship with people from all cultures and backgrounds. The church should reflect the beautiful diversity of the world.

Part 2:
SCRIPTURE

In Part 2, we will take a closer look at common questions about the Scriptures. When it comes to the Bible, rumors abound and misinformation runs rampant, so it's no surprise that the uninformed are easily confused. In these three chapters, we'll take a closer look at the most common questions people have about the Bible, and offer answers you can present to skeptics and seekers.

CHAPTER 4

Has the Bible Been Changed?

*O*ver the years I must have seen dozens of articles making claims like these: "The Bible's Been Changed!", or "The Bible Contains 50,000 Errors!" And sadly, many people will glance at a title like this, think to themselves, "I *knew* I couldn't trust that book," and never bother to investigate the validity of the claim.

Over the years, many allegations have been made about the translation, interpretation, and relevance of the Bible. One set of criticisms claims the Bible's message has been lost in translation, tampered with, or rewritten in accordance with the church's agenda. How seriously ought we to take such an accusation? And how should believers respond when talking with people who doubt the trustworthiness of the Bible?

The Bible is honest

First off, let's remind people that the Bible isn't the kind of story people would make up if they were just inventing a religion. If this were a merely human work, we'd expect the embarrassing and apparently contradictory parts to have been cut out, not left in. Yet we read—without censorship—of David's adultery and murder, Abraham's deceit and cowardice, Sarah's faithlessness and meanness, and Peter's impulsiveness and compromise.

Of course one (and only one) Bible hero is an exception to this: Jesus Christ, who is perfect (John 8:46). The candor of the Bible, especially with respect to its principal characters, gives strong reason to accept its overall veracity.

We can trust the translations

Another point we should make is that translators work from the best available copies, and we have compelling evidence to believe the scriptures we read today match those of millennia ago. The Dead Sea Scrolls demonstrate the fidelity of the Old Testament copyists over a thousand-year period. From 1947 to 1956, the Dead Sea Scrolls were uncovered in caves in Qumran, untouched since AD 68. Archaeologists uncovered copies of biblical manuscripts—every OT book is represented except Esther. Researchers spent some forty years painstakingly piecing the manuscripts together and translating them. The translations are amazingly similar to the versions of these books that we already had, showing the faithfulness of copyists over the years and proving that the Bible we read today is essentially the same Bible that people were reading one thousand years ago.

The 5500 Greek manuscripts (partial and complete) that still exist from before the printing press (the 1440s) suggest that the New Testament has also been well preserved.

Further, the charge that the Bible has been "copied so many times" (and presumably altered a bit every time) is demonstrably false. Many people picture translation going like this: the original Greek is rendered into Latin (before the Greek manuscript is lost forever), then the Latin translation is translated into Old English, then the Old English version is adapted into Middle and Modern English, and on and on it goes, each translation growing another layer distant from the original. But this isn't the way it works. All translations are translated *directly from the oldest available manuscripts* (Greek for the NT, Hebrew and Aramaic for the OT), and these parchments and papyri are ancient—up to 2200 years old (OT), or 1800 years old (NT). The Bibles we hold in our hands have been translated from the earliest possible manuscripts.

A lasting message

What can we conclude? The text of the Bible has been preserved adequately. Not perfectly—be careful not to over-commit yourself by claiming the manuscripts are error-free. (This is unnecessary for a claim of divine inspiration.) Yet sometimes critics claim that *any* error would require us to dismiss the entire Bible. But that's not the way history works. No ancient manuscript is perfectly preserved. Minor copying errors don't necessarily negate or "change" the document, any more than a typo invalidates a legal contract. The important thing is that the message has remained unchanged.

Points to Remember:

- Learn how to turn the potentially scandalous elements of Scripture into reasons to trust it: The biblical story isn't the sort of story anyone would just make up. If the church were fabricating the Bible, why highlight the sins of its prominent leaders? Transparency is a strong reason to trust the Bible's integrity. Further, few growth strategies would have been less promising than showcasing the disgraceful death of their founder. And yet that's precisely what the early Christians did (1 Cor 1:23)—and it was powerful!
- Translations are made from a wealth of ancient manuscripts, generally the oldest available, and they are accurate. There's no need to fear the message was lost through the course of copying.
- A minor copying error doesn't invalidate the entire message. In order to preserve the message, the copying process only needed to be adequate, not perfect. Expect your friends to value normal criteria for accessing the past—not exaggerated ones.

In conclusion, the Scriptures weren't twisted or changed. The only "twisting" is that done by people with self-serving interpretations (2 Pet 3:16).

CHAPTER 5

Dismissing the Word

Some assaults on the Bible are mean and ugly. Although other criticisms are softer and gentler, they serve to push people away from God's word just as effectively. What are some of these charges, and how can we answer them?

1. "The Bible is old-fashioned."

People accuse the Bible of being old-fashioned or out of date, perhaps meaningful in a bygone age but irrelevant to our present concerns. How to respond to this charge? God's word will never pass away (Matt 24:35); the principles always apply. A modern man might commit adultery in an air-conditioned hotel room with electric lighting and synthetic curtains, but it's still adultery. The betrayal, the guilt, the secrecy—all are common themes unchanged by time or technology. That is because people are the same, and our basic concerns remain constant (friendship, meaning, esteem, and so forth). Since the Bible is a book about relationships (with God and with others), it will always be relevant.

2. "It's all a matter of interpretation."

What does that mean? It's true, not because no one can figure out what the Bible is saying, but because in order to get the point we have to interpret carefully. (And this is true of *any* book—not just the Bible.) We must recognize grammar, logic, and figures of speech. Ignore grammar, take metaphor literally, and so on, and you can "prove" anything (though not necessarily what the biblical writer intended). Good interpreters respect context. They take into account that Scripture is thirty percent poetry (the rules of interpretation change when we go from prose to poetry). They don't rush through a passage trying to find support for their opinions. Good interpreters recognize that there are multiple ways to convey truth: narrative, letter, poem, hymn, apocalypse, and so on. So yes, it is a matter of interpretation: careful or careless. Which will we employ?

3. "Men wrote the Bible, so it's just the word of man—not the word of God."

The criticism suffers from two failings. First, this forces a false choice. God could just as easily relay his message through messengers as he could write it himself. A secretary's involvement in a memorandum doesn't diminish the boss's authority; one person is simply communicating through another. Tertius was technically the writer of Romans (Rom 16:22), yet the letter was still from Paul (Rom 1:1). The Bible is the word of man *and* the word of God. Second, the criticism is unrealistic. Humans learn and think in human languages, gaining insight by way of human illustrations. How else could God speak to us in an enduring way, if not in languages we can understand (or translate), through analogies we can relate to, and in documents preserved for future generations? The Bible is exactly the kind of book we might expect from a God who wishes to communicate with us!

Compliments that undermine the power of the Bible

Finally, the most subtle assaults on Scripture come by way of backhanded compliments. It's easier to call the Bible "good literature" than to live by it. In my part of the United States (Georgia), people call the Bible "the Good Book." Yet the truth is, the Bible is *so* good that the compliment is almost meaningless. For the Bible is stunning in its accuracy, penetrating in its insight, inspiring in its truthfulness and usefulness (2 Tim 3:16–17). And the Scriptures reveal God. I have observed that those who say "the Good Book" aren't generally the ones striving to master it.

At the bottom of a skeptic's resistance to the word—say, through tactics like those refuted here—may be their desire to live life with minimal accountability to any ultimate authority. The attitude of our generation matches that expressed by many in the time of the prophet Isaiah:

"Leave this way,
   get off this path,
and stop confronting us
   with the Holy One of Israel!" (Isa 30:11)

Points to Remember:

- "It isn't relevant": The Bible *is* relevant. Human nature hasn't changed, and our spiritual needs are the same as ever. God's word is no more out of date than water or oxygen!
- "It's all a matter of interpretation": The Bible requires careful interpretation, though not because it's ambiguous and up for grabs. There's only one other kind of interpretation—careless. We can agree that the Bible *is* a matter of interpretation: careful versus careless.
- "Men wrote it, so it isn't God's word": Scripture is the word of God *and* the word of man. It's not either/or, but both/and. Be aware when a critic is pressing you to make a false choice.
- "It's the Good Book": No, the Bible isn't "the Good Book." The Bible is the *best*, in a league of its own. It isn't just literature. In the Bible we hear God's voice calling us to a radical decision. Reject backhanded compliments, since they attempt to dilute the unique demands of Scripture.

CHAPTER 6

Conspiracy Theories

*C*over-ups at the highest levels of government. Plots afoot in the Vatican. Terrorist intrigues. Conspiracies seem to be everywhere, and we're drawn to them. They're pored over on tablets, devoured on the big screen, and endlessly analyzed in coffeehouses or wherever else people converse about interesting things (Acts 17:21).

Popular conspiracy theories about Christianity can easily dupe the uninformed. You probably don't need a degree in theology to refute these wild theories—just a few pointers. Although there are scores of religious conspiracies, at this time we'll touch on just three that call biblical authority into question:

1. Deletion of documents and mysterious material: Books have been removed from the Bible; the OT and NT Apocrypha.
2. Suppression of evidence: The Dead Sea Scrolls disprove Christianity.
3. Deliberate mistranslation: The true Bible (the King James Version) is under attack.

1. "Books have been removed from the Bible."

First, what about the so-called missing books? Thousands of documents were written before, during, and after biblical times—hardly surprising. So first off, we must be clear that ancient writings weren't "scripture" just because they dealt with matters of faith. The candidates for biblical material are surprisingly few, falling into two main groups.

First, when some people speak of missing books they're thinking of the Apocrypha, intertestamental literature (200 BC–AD 50) that was highly valued by the ancient church. Much of the Apocrypha is valuable, and whatever your view as to its inspiration, you will benefit from studying it.

Second, more recently it has become trendy to think that Christianity began with scores of competing apocryphal gospels, acts, letters, and apocalypses. This is easily disproved. Not one of these so-called "missing books" was ever part of the New Testament. In fact, these sectarian documents were written a century or two (or even longer) after the NT canon closed (about AD 95). These spurious documents frequently embellish, distort, or contradict the canonical NT. I hope that, as a biblical Christian, you will be motivated to learn the facts about how the Bible came to be.

2. "The Dead Sea Scrolls disprove Christianity."

A second common notion is that the Dead Sea Scrolls (DSS, discovered from 1947–1956, preserved in caves in what was then the nation of Jordan) disprove Christianity—for which reason they've been suppressed by the Vatican. But this is nonsense! If you aren't familiar with the fascinating story of the DSS, let's consider the basic facts (which are always better than fiction).[5] True, these scrolls—some complete but most in fragmentary condition—were not quickly published. Yet not because of a perfidious plot, but because (1) translation work was difficult and laborious, (2) the principal translators kept dying, and (3) publication lags behind translation when there are so few academics familiar with the ancient languages. Since 1992, all DSS have been translated and made public. They shed considerable light on ancient Judaism (most of the DSS date from 200 BC–AD 68), and hence illuminate—and often confirm—Christianity and the NT. The Hebrew DSS also give proof positive that the OT has been accurately preserved over the period of 2000–3000 years!

3. "The true Bible (the King James Version) is under attack."

Our third conspiracy is popular among some ultra-strict Christians. They claim that the only English Bible authorized by God is the King James Version of 1611—the perfect translation. Yet this is lazy thinking, oblivious of the actual history of translation. There were many English Bibles before the KJV, each generation offering up fresher, more accurate translations. No single generation can stake its claim to perfect English, for ours is a dynamic language, changing continuously for more than 1500 years! The KJV-only people also allege that liberal translators undermine the miracles and divinity of Christ, as modern versions (rightly) remove some words that crept into the text in the Middle Ages. No doctrine stands or falls on minor translation differences, anyway[6].

All three of these "conspiracies" fail on closer examination. Conspiracies are sometimes more juicy than historical truth, but as followers of the One who claimed to be the truth (John 14:6) we should always check our sources—or else we become part of the conspiracy. Don't be mesmerized by the sensational. Sometimes a conspiracy theory is just . . . a conspiracy.

Points to Remember:

- "Books have been removed from the Bible": These books were never in the Bible in the first place. These sectarian productions not only contradict the Scriptures, but were produced long after them. The Lord seems to be preserving his word, so that no one can add to it or take away from it (Matt 24:35; Jer 36:23, 32)!
- "The Dead Sea Scrolls disprove Christianity": The Scrolls disprove nothing, and actually illuminate the background of Judaism and Christianity. Moreover, they provide rock solid evidence that the oldest parts of the Bible (the Old Testament)

have been copied adequately; the message has been preserved through the millennia.

- "The only true Bible is the KJV": It wasn't a bad version for 1611 (ignoring five hundred errors corrected in the second edition), but it's out of date now. Besides, translators work from the oldest and best manuscripts. King James's men had no access to the nineteenth- and twentieth-century treasure troves: numerous NT Greek manuscripts (including 131 papyri), as well as hundreds of Hebrew Dead Sea Scrolls and other documentary finds.

Part 3:
MORALITY

Morality is an uncomfortable topic for many people today. Why? Because *morality* is a loaded word. Morality means there is right and there is wrong—and therefore you and I are sometimes right and sometimes wrong. (And if we are sometimes right and sometimes wrong, then we have things to feel guilty about, and we need saving after all!) Many people prefer "safer" terms like *values*, which are subjective, and allow us to escape without feelings of guilt. How can we discuss the concept of morality with our skeptical friends? In these chapters, we'll explain ways to help them understand the crucial difference between morals and values, and how the existence of morality supports the existence of God.

CHAPTER 7

Morality: "That's personal!"

Defining terms

In talking about morality, it may be helpful to define terms. Morality refers to the goodness of one's intentions or actions. Ethics relates to obligations towards others. Adapting C. S. Lewis' memorable illustration, think of a fleet of ships.[7] Morality means keeping our own ship seaworthy. We want our vessel to be clean, functional, and in good repair. Ethics is how our ship relates to other ships— keeping a safe distance, avoiding collision, communicating clearly, and so forth. So far, so good. Why would anyone object to these definitions?

Escape tactics

People object because they've been told virtue is out of vogue, to be dismissed as a relic of the Dark Ages. Modern society uses four tactics to wiggle out of morality:

1. **It rejects morals as antiquated.**
   Virtue and vice, righteousness and sin are old-fashioned. We've progressed beyond the primitive level of people in biblical times. Yet no one reading the Bible and the morning paper side by side would ever claim this, for they both describe the same dynamics.

2. **It replaces virtue with "values."**
   The vocabulary of virtue has suffered a serious downgrade. Originally, we were supposed to value what was valuable—not trash. When Plato spoke of "the good," or the preacher expounded on "sin," there was general agreement that good and evil are meaningful categories, and that words about good and evil are connected with a real moral world. No more! Instead of actions and lifestyle choices being good or evil, they become subjective "values"—which are private.

   People often say, "Virtues may be real for you, but they aren't for me." Educators, media pundits, film stars, and namby-pamby preachers have all bought into this attack on virtue. They seem to be terrified of being thought judgmental or bigoted, and are quick to parrot the vocabulary of the world.

3. **It separates private life from the public sphere.**
   Modern society naively imagines that one's private character shouldn't be taken into account when it comes to one's public life. Yet surely someone who has made thousands of little compromises is more likely, given something of importance to do (like run a company or a nation), to make a few big compromises. Further, a man who betrays his wife (adultery) may think little of selling out those who trust him to do what is right.

4. **It condones any behavior long as it doesn't "hurt" others.**
   At first this sounds somewhat reasonable. "Leave me alone—I'm not hurting anyone." But is this true?

   Moral choices affect everyone. Virtue has a leavening effect through society (Matt 5:13). Vice, like pollution, diminishes the quality of life for all us. Further, while all sins are not equal, all sins are serious, from the "little ones" to "big sins." We may be horrified by murder, but what about premarital sex? How about slander, or disrespect? All sin is a violation of God's will, and is destructive.

Let's develop this idea with several examples.

- A person may think, "I'm not hurting anyone by throwing this trash on the ground." But is littering harmless? We all pay: collectively by higher taxes, or aesthetically by being forced to behold ugliness in place of natural beauty.
- Now consider gluttony. Are there any victims besides the gourmand? Yes—higher health premiums affect us all.
- All crimes, from tax evasion to bank robbery, drive up the cost of living, even if it wasn't my bank that was robbed.
- Indulging in porn assures the victimization of a steady stream of young women (and men and even children).
- Even if a drunk isn't driving, his poor judgment still affects others: absenteeism in effect lowers our wages (we have to work harder to cover him); he probably hogs more than his fair share of health care, too.
- Gossip may seem trivial, but it unfairly affects how we view and interact with third parties.
- Academic cheating lowers educational standards, and confirms the cheater in patterns that may continue in the workplace.
- Materialism—the Bible calls it greed—feeds consumerism, which often furthers the exploitation of workers in the developing world.

Sin twists our character, saps our moral strength (virtue) and integrity, and weakens our love for others. Sin affects the individual (guilt), but it also has social consequences, like alienation. The most serious effect of sin is separation from God (Isa 59:1–3; Col 1:21). Any sin can be forgiven (except the one we refuse to repent from), but divine forgiveness doesn't obliterate sin's psychological, social, and spiritual consequences. The Bible tells us that our true problem isn't intellectual, but moral. Embracing "values" in lieu of the biblical diagnosis needs to be exposed for what it is. Only then will people realize their true need, and realize that the gospel is good news.

How to respond?

How might we respond when a nonbeliever, parroting the world's arsenal of excuses, defends unrighteous behavior? People make three common excuses:

1. **"It's my choice."**
   Agree. We take choices seriously, and are glad our friend recognizes his decisions are his own responsibility. But that doesn't end the discussion; keep going.

2. **"It's none of your business."**
   This is somewhat true. Your friend's choices may not immediately concern you. But they may be his wife's business (say, if he has violated his wedding vows). His moral character may affect his children, his neighbors, his boss . . .

3. **"It's okay, as long as I'm not hurting anyone."**
   As we have seen, what's done in private affects the public. A man may smoke cigarettes at home, and may even be considerate when it comes to secondhand smoke. But consider how health care costs are driven up by the choice to smoke! To return to the marine analogy, you might reply, "Your private sin makes it all the more likely that one day your ship will crash into mine!"

Ultimately . . .

Ultimately, all sin is between each person and God. Most sin affects other people, directly or indirectly. But since every sin is an offense against the Lord (Gen 39:9; Ps 51:4), it's simply not true that poor moral choices don't hurt anyone else.

Morals police?

Our responsibility as evangelistic Christians is to speak the truth in love, in the hope that our friend will come to a knowledge of the truth (Eph

4:15, 25; 2 Tim 2:23–26). We aren't the morals police, nor is there any place for a superior attitude.

When it comes to morality, we ought to be hardest on ourselves (we have the least excuse for our own behavior, because we have the Bible as our guide)—and gracious towards others. Yet true grace doesn't mean buying into the excuses and deflections the world uses to hide from God (John 3:19–21).

Points to Remember:

- In desiring to live free from God's authority, our world is trying to replace virtue with "values." But "values" are subjective; you prefer or approve a certain behavior. Your value isn't right or wrong—although it may be "right" for you. No wonder, loosed from its moral moorings, the human race is adrift in a sea of relativity (Eccl 7:29).
- When we act in violation of God's will, we sin against God. Of course in a god-less world this wouldn't be the case—but then there'd be no morality, only preference. Since Christ died for us, we should never take sin lightly (Heb 10:26–31).
- Sin also affects others, even if it is committed in private. Sin diminishes our capacity to love. It erodes character. Like certain beverages and medications, it influences judgment—sooner or later somebody is going to be hurt (Gal 5:19–26).

CHAPTER 8

The Euthyphro Dilemma

In this chapter we examine the Euthyphro Dilemma, a philosophical argument sometimes used by atheists to discredit faith. Though it will be most familiar to university students, every Christian thinker should be prepared with an answer to the dilemma. The Bible encourages all of us to be on our guard against specious arguments: "I say this in order that no one may delude you with plausible arguments. . . . See to it that no one takes you captive by philosophy and empty deceit." (Col 2:4, 8 ESV).

Here's the dilemma: Is something good because God has commanded it, or has God commanded it because it is good?[8]

Is God arbitrary, or not ultimate?

Let's unpack this. On the one hand, if something is good simply because God says so, then good is arbitrary. What makes something right is God's approval, not any objective, inherent quality of goodness. We may recognize an act as good or evil, but God could have commanded otherwise. For example, he might have declared that the highest virtue is petting dogs, or shaving one's head. As for vice, if all it takes is a divine decree, then God might have forbidden charity as evil.

On the other hand, if God commands only because something is good, then God isn't ultimate, since good already exists apart from him. God himself would be required to obey the moral law—implying this law is above/greater than him. In both cases, the God of the Bible (who is ultimate, absolute, and good) wouldn't exist, since his decrees would be either arbitrary or redundant. How to escape the dilemma?

Some philosophers think one cannot escape Plato's logic. Yet in fact we're being asked to accept one of two false choices: morality exists apart from God, or God's moral commands are arbitrary.

Morality rooted in the nature of God

Good is good not because of any decree, or because good exists apart from the Deity, but because it conforms with God's nature. No command is needed to make something right or wrong (although we do benefit from God's wisdom revealed in his word). If morality is determined by the character of God, there is no true dilemma. We are right to reject both false choices. The dilemma is a trick—a good example of bad philosophy.

Imitate Jesus' sharp mind

Jesus wasn't one to be cornered and trapped by words. In fact, he was masterful at navigating dilemmas (Mark 11:27–33, 12:13–16). Let's imitate him!

And you never know—the solution to the Euthyphro Dilemma might come in handy some day. The solution is also useful since it drives us to recognize the holiness and transcendence of the infinitely good God.

Points to Remember:

- No philosophy can disprove God. It is a futile exercise to attempt to disprove God!
- God's commands are neither arbitrary nor superfluous.
- God's nature itself is the standard of goodness. D. A. Carson put it well: "The dimensions of evil are thus established by the dimensions of God; the ugliness of evil is established by the

beauty of God; the filth of evil is established by the purity of God; the selfishness of evil is established by the love of God."[9]

CHAPTER 9

Is God Dead?

G od is dead and we have killed him," wrote Friedrich Nietzsche
(1844–1900). Nietzsche's famous dictum doesn't mean that God
once existed but now lives no more. "God is dead" refers to the
functional significance of God for morality and ethics. Without a God,
there is no way to speak of true morality.

I'm not just regurgitating something I read about this philosopher.
Last year I read his *Beyond Good and Evil*—pretty astounding. I
came across such bold assertions as "There is no such thing as moral
phenomena, but only a moral interpretation of phenomena," and also,
"The whole of morality is a long, audacious falsification."[10] No wonder
he was Hitler's favorite philosopher.

What Nietzsche meant was that the old world (God, absolutes,
morality) is gone. We have undone it. If there's no God, then it's pointless
to talk about right and wrong. There is no morality in a godless world.
With this at least the thinking Christian should agree!

Nietzsche's predictions for the twentieth century (he died in the
last year of the nineteenth) were spot on. He foresaw that the world,
morally unhinged, would go crazy, ending up awash in blood. Indeed,
a pall of insanity descended on our planet, and the levels of violence we

reached—often justified by godless or atheistic ideologies—dwarfed all previous centuries, with over 200 million dead (39 million dead in wars, 169 million in state-sponsored genocide, execution, and persecution).

In short, Nietzsche taught: No God, no morality. Nothing is right or wrong; it just is what it is.

While we can agree that without God the world descends into chaos and sin, and loses all sense of morality, as Christians we hold that God *does* exist, and is still very much at work in this world. His rules, his definition of morality, and his authority still stand—even if the world chooses to ignore them. Those who ignore God's ways pay a painful price, and we see those consequences at work daily in our world.

Points to Remember:

- By his famous saying, "God is dead," Nietzsche meant not that God has expired, but that he is functionally dead. The Judeo-Christian God, the all-knowing, all-powerful, and all-good Judge, has lost his authority. We've advanced beyond any need for him.
- If atheism is true, then nothing is absolutely good or evil, since there's no absolute standard by which to measure morality. In short, no God, no morality.

CHAPTER 10
Why Morality Means God

*I*n the past few chapters we have been examining morality. Opinions run strong, yet God's word is clear: there are universal moral absolutes in this world—certain non-negotiable truths that no amount of philosophizing can get around. Sure, there's some gray in the world (gray areas, gray hair, and gray matter, to name a few). Yet there's also black and white. Right and wrong aren't simply a matter of preference, like favorite flavors of ice cream, which are subjective (not objective).

While people may have occasional disagreements over some moral or ethical issues, everyone agrees that some things are always wrong—like torturing babies for fun. And I've never met a skeptic who didn't think it absolutely wrong to coerce others to convert. What kind of a world would this be without true good (love, grace, integrity, and so on)? A world where serial killers received praise, while honest persons were censured? Our general agreement on the existence of certain moral absolutes readily feeds into one of the strongest evidences that there is a God.

Syllogism

Let's now approach the matter from a philosophical perspective, making use of a syllogism. The first syllogism I ever heard, in a junior high school English class, was:

1. All men are mortal.
2. Socrates is a man.
3. Therefore Socrates is mortal.

The conclusion follows from the premises. So if the premises are true, the conclusion must also be true.

Let's consider another syllogism, which is a proof for God:

1. If there's no God, then there are no universal, objective moral values.
2. Objective moral values do in fact exist.
3. Therefore, God exists.

Let's analyze the argument:
1. If there's no universal good by which actions can be measured, then we may speak of preferences or opinions, but not of objective values.
2. Objective morals do exist, and nearly anyone will concede the point.
3. The conclusion follows directly from the premises: God exists.

The value of universal standards

Let's step a step back from our discussion of morality, and consider the idea of universal standards in general. Without them, how could anyone measure anything? I normally weigh 100 kg. But what if at my friend's house I tip the scales at 150 kg? Somebody's scales need recalibrating—but whose? We can't appeal to either scale to settle the matter; we need a third scale, one we both agree is accurate. Similarly, without an external moral standard, who's to say something is good or evil? If there's no God, then there is (ultimately) no morality. We are "beyond good and evil" (Nietzsche). "Whatever is, is right" (the Marquis de Sade). The world is an ugly place, without God and without hope (Eph 2:12).

Persuasion

For these reasons, we who live by faith have a mandate to distinguish right from wrong in our own lives, and to teach others. We can use the syllogism presented here to convince our erudite friends. If they get stuck on the second premise, keep pushing. Eventually they will almost certainly acknowledge its truth.

Of course we can't force anyone to believe in God. They always have a choice. Back to the syllogism for a moment. Nietzsche would have heartily endorsed the first premise: If there's no God, then there are no universal, objective moral values. He would also agree with the conclusion—that the syllogism is valid and God exists. What he would reject is premise 2, the existence of any objective, universal morality. He foresaw that without morality, the world would go crazy (his prediction for the twentieth century, as well as his own experience—he died insane). No one was meant to pilot his ship without a compass. Without the moral compass of God and his word, we are on a collision course with reality. That's why "we persuade men" (2 Cor 5:11).

Points to Remember:

- Since true morality can only exist in a world with God, God truly exists.
- This may be demonstrated through a simple syllogism, which constitutes powerful evidence for God's existence.
- Note: We're not saying that an atheist can't act morally, or that only Christians are good people. We are saying that *no one* can be moral in a world without morality—and that is the only world possible if there is no God.

Part 4:
GOD

In Part 4, we will explore objections to God made by doubters, seekers, atheists, and agnostics. Does God exist? Does the Judeo-Christian concept of God make sense? If God does exist, what is he like, and is he worth following?

CHAPTER 11
The Old Man in the Sky

*H*ow can you Christians believe in an Old Man in the Sky?" You may have been asked that question, and you probably replied, "We don't." The common caricature of God is ridiculous. Atheists and Christians hold similar reasons for rejecting the concept, and this common ground has the potential to open up many profitable lines of discussion.

All the following questions make the same assumption. Can you tell what that assumption is?

- "How can God possibly hear millions of prayers at the same time?"
- "What race is God?"
- "Is God male or female?"
- "Why does he want to spoil our fun?"
- "The Bible says he's a jealous God. What's his problem?"
- "The Bible says he's angry. Isn't such behavior inappropriate for a being with all knowledge and all power? And eternal torture— what a barbarian!"

- "Why should God need our worship? Is he insecure?"
- "Why does the Bible say God regretted creating mankind?"

Human limitations

What underlies each question is an assumption that God shares our limitations. It's a view of God as a slightly more advanced version of ourselves. Yet if the true God is the one described in the Bible—spirit, not flesh; personal, but not human; real, though not bound by space-time—then each question is easily answered.

If all times are equally accessible to God, then he has all eternity to consider our prayers. He isn't black or white, because he's not a human. Nor is he male or female. Both genders express his image, and yet God is not sexual.[11] He isn't some senile, doting grandfather—or the opposite, a cranky killjoy, too old to have fun. Besides, outside time is there aging? We can't pull a fast one on God, as he is all-knowing. And his aim isn't to smother us, but to offer us life to the full (John 10:10).

There are many passages that refer to the "arm" or "eyes" of the Lord in order to express his power, knowledge, and so forth. This is called anthropomorphic language—*anthropos* (human) + *morphē* (form)—language that's been accommodated to our human level of thinking, so that we can relate to God. For example, when the Lord walks in the Garden of Eden in the cool of the day and asks Adam, "Where are you?", we shouldn't think God has lost track of Adam, any more than that his presence in the Garden means he isn't omnipresent (immanent in the entire cosmos).

Many skeptics seem to assume that jealousy is unworthy of divinity, but it is not. Shouldn't we husbands jealously guard our wives? Surely we shouldn't share them with other men. Is anger always wrong? Shouldn't God be angry with the perpetrators of genocide? In fact, if he weren't jealous and angry, he would not be God. There is no reason to think that divine anger or jealousy is tinged with selfishness, as it so often is in our case.

As for the accusation that God subjects sinners to nonstop, infinite torture—there are strong reasons for rejecting this notion. God is just, so if anyone deserves punishment, it will be fair (Luke 12:47–48).[12]

God doesn't need our worship; the need lies wholly on our side. When we are improperly oriented to the king of the universe, we are filled with deceitful pride and bring harm to ourselves and to others. Worship is the natural response of the creature in the presence of its creator. As for God's "regretting" creating mankind (some versions of Gen 6:6 say "repenting," though "relenting" is a better word), God's pain at our sin involves no element of surprise, as though the Deity were caught off guard. (He knew it was coming.) Yet he feels pain because his relationship with us is actual, not fictive.

This is only a smattering of questions and responses. All these points can be backed up with scriptures. I have discovered that most atheists are taken aback when they first hear a reasonable portrayal of God. Sometimes at this point they look away, realizing that their first line excuses is weaker than they'd supposed.

So how should we respond to the atheist who declines to believe in "the Old Man in the Sky"?

- Where possible, agree with your friend! The Old Man in the Sky turns out to be a straw man—on this you both agree. You have something in common.
- Gently correct them, with the goal to help them to reimagine what the true God is like.
- Commend them where their insights are "biblical." Get them to think outside the box. Ask, "What kind of a God could you believe in?" Your friend may be closer to the kingdom than you realize.
- Emphasize that the God of the Bible is spirit, not flesh; personal, yet not subject to human weakness; and somehow above (not trapped in) space and time.

Points to Remember:

- Sometimes unbelievers protest that they don't believe in "the Old Man in the Sky." We should heartily agree. The caricature depicts nothing more than a superhero with human limitations (think Zeus, Jupiter, or Thor)—a god made in man's image.

When we agree with our friends on this point, not only do we disarm them, but we are also able to contrast inferior concepts of God with what we know of the true God.

- A reasonable concept of God is found in Scripture: an infinite being who operates outside space-time; who is spirit, not flesh; and who is personal, though without human weakness. He is almighty, all-knowing, everywhere present, holy, righteous, and good.

CHAPTER 12

You Say There's a God? Prove It!

Sometimes skeptics demand proof of God. But what sort of proof are they looking for? Usually they are seeking empirical (scientific) proof. Yet there are other kinds of "proof." In a court of law, forensic evidence isn't always a photo, fiber, or matching DNA. Eyewitness testimony can be highly persuasive. So can the triple conjunction of motive, means, and opportunity.

Insisting on empirical (scientific) proof when God is an immaterial being is itself illogical! Many things cannot be empirically proven, yet are real nonetheless: logic, numbers, justice, love, beauty, and science itself.

For example:

- The axioms of logic, as of geometry, must be assumed. They cannot be proven. Using logic to prove logic would be circular. Some element of faith is therefore involved at the fundamental level.
- Numbers, whether integers or fractions or those special numbers like e and i and π, are well known to all of us. Mathematics is the "language" of physics (formulas, ratios, coefficients, etc.),

and numbers make up the "words." Even though numbers are useful to scientists, their existence cannot be proven—not even by the scientists who use them.

- Justice and love are real—all of us demand or seek them!—yet they cannot be quantified. Who ever heard of 2 kg of justice, or 12 cc of love?
- Beauty, whether artistic or musical, speaks powerfully to every person. Even though we cannot always define beauty—the attempt tends to be clunky and detracts from the object of our admiration—we experience it as real.
- Like logic, science is not self-verifying. There are always assumptions. Thus we see that many things in our world are real (miracles also fall into this category), even though they cannot be proved empirically.

I am often asked how we as believers can "prove God." We cannot prove him scientifically, but this is no problem, as we now understand that much of reality is beyond the reach of empirical analysis. It is possible to experience God and to persuade others of his existence, yet there is no way scientifically to prove God.

The universe indicates intelligence and personality
Even though we can't prove God, we find evidence for him everywhere. The universe displays profound complexity: everything that is has come about through processes following natural laws that can be reduced to elegant mathematical formulas. These intricacies suggest a brilliant mastermind. In addition to intelligence, the world also displays personality. Surely it is more likely that a universe exhibiting intelligence and personality originated in an intelligent personal being than in impersonal matter and energy!

We have moderate evidence
Skeptics who ask us to prove God are dissatisfied with the amount of evidence God has given: it's moderate, not overwhelming. But is this necessarily a point against biblical faith? I think not.

Faith is not only a response to evidence, but also trust in a higher power. And faith is relational. Several centuries ago the philosopher and mathematician Blaise Pascal (1623–1662) had an exquisite insight: "[God] so regulates the knowledge of himself that he has given some signs of himself, visible to those who seek him and not to those who seek him not. There is enough obscurity for those who have a contrary disposition."[13]

In other words, the amount of evidence God provides of his existence is moderate—just right. He neither overwhelms the seeker with signs of his reality, nor provides so little evidence that anyone can reject him with good reason. The Lord respects our free will. He could force us to believe, yet he refuses to disrespect us. It is only in providing a moderate amount of evidence that our response can properly combine free will, rational response, and trust.

The Creator is set apart from his creation

God may not be provable scientifically, yet this doesn't mean he isn't real. Many things in the real world are beyond the reach of science, which after all only explores the realm of matter and energy in space-time. If God were scientifically verifiable, he would be in some sense part of the physical world—which would make him part of the creation, as opposed to the Creator who by definition exists outside of and apart from his creation. Finally, maybe God doesn't want us to be able to prove him. This allows for faith and a free will response. Thus what may have seemed a weakness in the biblical position turns out to be a great strength!

Points to Remember:

- There are many kinds of evidence. Though "evidence" may suggest scientific proof, much of the world lies outside the scope of science. Many things cannot be measured empirically (number, logic, beauty, justice, etc.), yet that doesn't mean they aren't real. To insist on scientific evidence for God is misguided, since God is spirit (John 4:24), not flesh.

- Although nobody can "prove" God scientifically, abundant evidence points to God. The universe displays profound complexity, reflecting intelligence and personality.
- God has given us a moderate amount of evidence for his existence. Had he given us much more, we might well feel coerced to believe; had he given us much less, we might walk away and feel justified doing so. As with Goldilocks' porridge, it's the middle value that best meets the need.

CHAPTER 13

Concepts of God that Don't Work

The picture of God revealed in Scripture, as well as in the person of Jesus Christ, is stunning, intriguing, inspiring, overwhelming. We should be careful not to detract from our sense of mystery, or from our humility (the only proper response to such a being). Yet the biblical picture of God is also rational. It makes sense. Not so with the many man-made concoctions. Rather than accept that the Lord has made us in his image, humans on the whole have attempted to shape him in our image.

We've already considered the typical "human god" (the Old Man in the Sky), and rejected it roundly. Now let's discuss a few more man-made deities.

- **The Force:** Some people deride the notion of a personal God. They imagine it more sensible to believe in some kind of "force." This energy field courses through the universe and has a good side and a dark side, kind of like "the Force" depicted in the *Star Wars* films. The problem with this notion is that in the real world, forces don't *create*. Imagine a tornado creating a town, or a flood creating life; that's not going to happen. Nor are forces good or evil; they just *are*. So "the Force" has significantly less explanatory power than the biblical notion of a moral God who creates, loves, and empowers.

- **Idols:** Sometimes idols are the human gods we have already dismissed. Other times in human history these divinities have been animals, or surreal hybrids of human and animal or monster. Biblically speaking, even a fallacious concept of Christ is an "idol" (1 John 5:21; 2 Cor 11:1–4). Sometimes we make idols out of misplaced priorities—we "worship" whatever is most important to us. This "god" isn't necessarily religious, but we worship it by prioritizing it above all else, thinking about it all the time and making enormous sacrifices to get more of it.[14] We may be controlled by the god of sex, wealth (mammon), or a thousand other objects or activities or experiences that dominate our lives. But all idols fall short of the biblical God, and it is not without reason that they are frequently the targets of sarcastic critique (Isa 44:6–20).

- **I am God:** Under the influence of Eastern Religions and the New Age Movement, many people have been flattered into believing they are divine. In this view, our fundamental problem is not sin, but ignorance. Once we're enlightened about our true divine nature, the world will bend to our wishes. Yet if we are all God, then why do we disagree and fight (Jas 4:1–3)? Isn't there a better explanation (the biblical one)—that ego and self and sin are the problem, and repentance the solution? We get ourselves into a mess not because we are gods unaware of our powers, but because we're headstrong humans who want to be gods (Gen 3:1–5).

- **The state as god (totalitarianism):** Even in secular or atheist states, quasi-religious systems have resulted. The state, or its leadership, takes the place of God. Yet no person or institution or system has the right to demand our total loyalty—even if, and especially if, the institution is religious in nature. For whenever governments have made exclusive claims over the minds and hearts of their citizens, the natural results have been duplicity, injustice, violence, and a culture of fear. (Think Cambodia, Cuba, or the Soviet Union.)

None of these concepts match up with the God we encounter in the Bible and through Jesus Christ. The true God is rational (the biblical concept makes sense), relational (he's not just a power, but a being who interacts with his creatures), and righteous (since he's holy, his will often does not gibe with our own selfish preferences). In the end, he is the only God who makes sense!

Points to Remember:

- Idols leave us empty; they cannot fill the God-shaped void in our hearts.
- "The Force" has far less explanatory value than the Old Man in the Sky, since impersonal energy cannot account for personality, morality, or intelligence.
- Nothing has the right to claim our total loyalty except for God himself, which means that Christians can never go along with totalitarianism.
- New Age mysticism is silly. We are not God, despite the divine claims of the people flattered by this elitist fantasy.
- All "gods" are doomed to fail; they aren't real, nor does it makes sense to serve them. The God we encounter in the Bible and through Christ is the only one who makes sense!

CHAPTER 14

Coming to Terms: Defining Atheism and Agnosticism

*H*ow should you react when someone tells you, "Sorry, I'm an atheist"? Or what about when the person you were hoping to share the gospel with proclaims, "I'm an agnostic"? The goal of this chapter is to orientate us. First, a few key points about atheism and agnosticism, so that we know what we're dealing with.

Atheism

Atheism—*a* (not) + *theism* (belief in *theós*, God)—isn't a real position, but an *anti-position*. Nothing is positively affirmed, and this is its weakness. One exception suffices to disprove it. Theists hold that there is a God, an all-present, all-powerful, all-knowing being. Atheists hold that nowhere in the universe is there such a being. Yet in order to *know* that *nowhere* in the universe is there such a being, the atheist requires complete knowledge of the universe. He would need to be that which he denies—a being with universal knowledge! And again, a *single instance* of God's presence or activity refutes atheism in its entirety.

There are at least three types of atheists:

- **Type 1:** Most atheists simply assert that there is no God; they haven't really thought the matter through, and when challenged for their reasons, they either change the subject or plead ignorance.
- **Type 2:** Others have given the matter some thought. Most of these atheists resort to a blend of the various criticisms we have previously addressed, often with ad hominem attacks on believers. Yet such an approach hardly disproves God. Harping on the faults of Christians, insinuating that modern science overturns Scripture, or bringing up the scandal of the Crusades doesn't amount to much of an argument. They may well discredit some Christians, but this hardly discredits Christianity.
- **Type 3:** A small minority of atheists are serious thinkers, for instance several whom I have debated.[15] In order to win their respect—and hopefully nudge them towards a biblical understanding of God—you'll need to familiarize yourself with the wide spectrum of Christian apologetics.

Backwards reasoning

Apart from a handful of well-informed atheists, most unbelievers have arrived at their position through what I call backwards reasoning. That is, they find atheism comforts them, so they adopt it as their position, then go back and try to fill the gaps in their position. For example, maybe Christianity cramps their style (perhaps they are sexually active even though they are unmarried, or they may be put off by the notion of a day of judgment), and so they declare their atheism. Then they get busy seeking reasons to justify their newfound position. Or perhaps their peer group rejects church and morality and they want to fit in, so they give Confucius a cursory reading, grab a few sound bites from a documentary on the "missing" books of the Bible, and fold in some of their own speculations.

In all fairness, believers sometimes do the same thing, whether they are born into a faith family or come to faith in Christ later on. They're seeking justification for a position they've already embraced. Obviously, if you want to be thorough in your consideration of eternal matters, such an approach is defective.

Agnosticism

Like the word *atheism*, *agnosticism* also comes from the Greek: *a* (not) + *gnostós* (known). Agnostics contend that God is either unknown or unknowable. Christian apologists recognize two flavors of agnosticism:

- **Hard agnosticism:** "God is unknowable." This is the more philosophical of the two versions, yet it makes some unwarranted assumptions. It rules out experience of God; any supernatural experience is simply explained away. Agnosticism correctly recognizes that a God would be infinitely above the comprehension of finite man, yet it fails to consider that the infinite God might purpose to reach down to us humans (John 1:1–2, 14). Christians agree that God is unknowable exhaustively, yet they have experienced him in part. There is a difference between (some) knowledge of God and comprehensive, exhaustive knowledge of him. To illustrate, I have been married thirty years, but in one sense I'm still getting to know my wife. How much more is this the case in knowing the infinite God!

- **Soft agnosticism:** "I don't know if there's a God." This is seldom little more than lazy thinking. Of course not all agnostics are lazy. Some are actively seeking answers, aiming to put together the pieces. In this case, though, soon enough he or she will come to a conclusion, relinquishing the state of temporary ignorance. Oddly enough, I've met many (soft) agnostics who fancy themselves to be seekers, yet are not seeking in the biblical sense (Matt 7:7–8; Heb 11:6). They are not studying, thinking, and asking questions with the intention of making an informed decision. We should distinguish between intellectual modesty ("I don't have all the answers") and intellectual lethargy ("I may make a short-lived effort to seek now and again").

Other terms to know (which might come up in serious discussion):
- **Theism:** belief in a personal God. Christians and Jews are theists.

- **Deism:** belief in an impersonal God who created the cosmos but then stepped back and is no longer involved. He neither works miracles nor answers prayers. This was the position of many Enlightenment thinkers, as well as of many of the Founding Fathers of the United States.
- **Pantheism:** God is everywhere and everything; the world itself is divine. This is the view espoused by the New Age Movement, borrowed from such Eastern religions as Hinduism and Buddhism.
- **Polytheism:** belief in many gods.
- **Monotheism:** belief in one god.

Responses

So how can we engage atheists and agnostics in productive conversation? Here are a few ideas.

If someone is an atheist:

- Find out how long he's been an atheist, and why he thinks as he does. Has he lost his faith, or never had it? What does he think about "church people"? Ask lots of questions, and listen.
- Where appropriate, utilize the information in this chapter, and draw on other material from *Answering Skeptics*.
- Inquire about his relationship with his parents, especially his father. Most of us conceive of God as a heavenly father, extrapolating from our perception of our earthly parent. A harsh or distant father doesn't model God as he truly is. A relationship with a warm, nourishing father (1 Thess 2:6–12) creates a climate in which faith easily grows.
- If he/she asks you a tough question, don't change the subject. Answer it, or else admit that you don't know and promise to get back to him/her later with an answer.

If someone is an agnostic:

- Some of the responses for atheists may also be appropriate for your agnostic friends.

- **Hard agnostics:** Agree that in some sense God would be unknowable had he not taken the initiative to communicate with us. The Bible informs us that certain things may be known about God from nature, but other qualities are only known from Scripture, his relationship with Israel in the Old Testament, and the life and death of Jesus Christ. Show them from the Scriptures that in Christ, God has personally taken the initiative.
- **Soft agnostics:** Since they admit their ignorance, ask them, "Why not sort this out?" Offer your help in guiding them through the issues.

For both atheists and agnostics:
- Expose them to the biblical storyline. Help them to realize that the Bible isn't a book of rules, but an (unfinished) story about God, humans, and our place in his world.
- Patiently build a relationship with your atheist friend. Although Christianity has an intellectual side—and we are called to relate to God with all our mind (Mark 12:30; Luke 10:27)—it is the relational aspect that wins most people to Christ.
- Pascal's Wager may come in handy. The philosopher Pascal reasoned: It makes sense to believe in God, for if it turns out that there is a God yet we haven't believed in him, we stand to lose everything; if there isn't a God and we believe in him, in the long term we have lost nothing; yet if we believe in him and he exists, we have gained everything. Nothing to lose, everything to gain. I found the Wager especially useful in evangelism during my university years. Of course a biblical leap of faith isn't a decision to believe in spite of the lack of evidence, but faith is involved in our response to evidence.
- Remind them of what Jesus said in John 7:17: "Anyone who chooses to do the will of God will find out whether my teaching comes from God or whether I speak on my own." We won't find the answers through discussion alone; we must be willing to *act* on the evidence. Ask your friend, "If it turns out that what Jesus taught is true, would you be wiling to live the rest of your life

for him?" If he/she cannot reply in the affirmative, you know the bottom-line issue isn't intellectual. It's moral.

Points to Remember:

- **Atheist:** One who denies the existence of God. Point out to him that this anti-position cannot be proved, and share why you believe Christianity is true and reasonable.
- **Theist:** One who affirms the existence of God. Christians are theists.
- **Hard agnostic:** One who claims that God is unknowable (whether he exists or not). Focus on God's initiative in revealing himself to us.
- **Soft agnostic:** One who does not know whether God exists. Encourage them to have the integrity to be true seekers.

CHAPTER 15
Nonsense Questions

*I*n this chapter, we'll address some trick questions skeptics use to "prove" that the concept of God is illogical. Skeptics call them "contradictions"; I call them nonsense questions! The questions usually sound something like this:

If there's really a God . . .
- could he create loud silence?
- could he make a square circle?
- could he make a rock so heavy that even he couldn't lift it?

In each case, the skeptic expects a no answer. (And he's right; of course the answer is no.) But then the skeptic declares that God isn't all-powerful, since he is unable to accomplish these tasks. The all-powerful God is mere fiction.

Distinguishing sense from nonsense
We may sense that something is not quite right with the questions. It's not so much that they impugn God as that they play with our heads. Sometimes taking a moment to reflect on the problem allows us to

clarify the question. We need perspective. Here's my suggestion: Think, then reword.

Think: Loud silence is impossible by definition, since loud silence isn't silent. How can non-silence be silence? Unless one tinkers with definitions, or subverts logic, the combination is absolutely impossible. Even infinite power can't overthrow logic. The concept is incoherent.

Reword: Loud silence could be reworded "non-silent silence." That would violate the simple law of identity (A = A). The revised query becomes: Could God create non-silent silence?

Put this way, the question is exposed for what it is: a trick. The same goes for the square circle. How about the impossibly heavy rock? It's another nonsense question. An infinitely powerful God could move any rock—granted. But he could not exceed his own infinite powers in creating an even more infinite chunk of stone, for this would require that ∞ > ∞, which is mathematically impossible. (Sorry, God is unable to make 2 + 2 = 5, either.) If you prefer a simpler answer (of the tongue-in-cheek variety), you can respond: "Maybe not, but he could certainly make a bulldozer powerful enough to do the job."

Two kinds of impossibility

Biblically speaking, nothing is impossible for God (Luke 1:37). Yet what the critic asks not only does not exist, but *could not possibly* exist. Silence precludes sound, just as circularity precludes the right angles of the quadrilateral. Loud silences and square circles are impossible by definition. This first type of possibility is logical impossibility. The moment we assume these kinds of impossibilities, we are playing with words. We're not doing any serious thinking at all.

Of course there are countless things possible for God but impossible for us, or possible for one person but impossible for another. Unlike him, we cannot be in all places at all times. Nor as I type these words can I be in Atlanta, and in Copenhagen, where you might be reading them. When something is possible for God but impossible for us, we might call this relative impossibility. (You might not want to call it that, since I made up the term, and a real philosopher might well shred it to pieces!) Absolute impossibility is always impossible, no matter how powerful God is.

Is anything impossible for God?

The Bible tells us it is impossible for God to lie (Heb 6:18). He cannot violate his own nature, in this case not because he lacks power, but because he lacks evil. His nature is unchanging (Mal 3:6); he will always be omniscient, omnipotent, omnipresent, omnibenevolent (all good), and so on. The fact that God cannot lie seems related to the fact that he can't suspend the laws of logic, or make mathematical errors, or cause himself not to exist. So when Christians say that God accomplishes impossible things, we mean that he does the relatively impossible, not the absolutely impossible, which is meaningless.

He catches the wise in their craftiness

I wouldn't worry too much about the terms. I would be concerned, however, if someone was trying to pull the wool over my eyes. So next time someone asks you a question like these, take a moment. Think about what kind of question it is. It may well be a nonsense question, one that once reworded turns out to be meaningless. Then think of the scripture, "God catches the wise in their craftiness" (1 Cor 3:19; Job 5:13). Don't get drawn in to a foolish conversation that's been deliberately designed to go nowhere.

Jesus had a brilliant ability to respond to questions, criticism, and potential traps (see Luke 20:20–26). Together let's learn to "demolish arguments . . . and take captive every thought" (2 Cor 10:5).

Points to Remember:

- Many nonsense questions aim to discredit the classical concept of God by negating his omnipotence.
- Nothing is impossible for God (Luke 1:37), yet this passage refers to things that are logical or meaningful. There are some things God cannot do—not because he lacks power, but because those things are logically impossible (like creating "loud silence").

- When nonsense questions are reworded, they are exposed as meaningless (no one can create non-silent silence, and it is meaningless as a concept). God sees through such clever questions, and we should too (Job 5:13; 1 Cor 3:19; 2 Cor 10:5; Col 2:4).

Part 5:
SCIENCE

In this section we will take a look at questions about how science and nature relate to the Bible. Thinking people are often presented with a false choice: accept the Bible or believe in science—you can't do both. But science is *not* at odds with Scripture—in fact, the two are friends! Science grants us insights into the artistry and majesty of God, and causes us to stand even more in awe of him. We must learn to understand how God intends us to read and apply his written word, and how he wants us to view the world he has designed for us.

In these chapters, we will explore the main topics of debate, and strive to clear up the confusion and conflict. We'll cover questions about creation and its Creator; the Bible's relationship to science; the age of the earth; what Genesis *really* says (and doesn't say); and evolution.

Is it possible to believe in the Bible, and still learn from science? Absolutely. Let's find out how.

CHAPTER 16

Creation Questions

We begin our section on science and the Bible by examining questions related to creation in general. Let's take a look at some of the most common objections, and also explore a cosmological argument that will help you reason with your skeptical friends.

"The world is eternal, so there is no need for a creator."
The atheist may say, "You believe God has always existed. I say the world has always existed—no creator required—so we're even." How should we respond?

This one is easily answered. The conclusion of physicists and astrophysicists is that the world has not always existed. The current view (as of 2016) is that the world of time and space, matter and energy came into existence about 13.8 billion years ago. In other words, nothing became something. Thus the *something* has not always existed. The evidence that the cosmos had a beginning is the Big Bang, in which the entire universe exploded out of nothing.

In fact, the "creation" (the term scientists often employ) strongly suggests that there is a God. Otherwise, how can we account for the world, especially with its degree of intricacy, apparent design (intelligence), and personality?

It is sometimes imagined that, given sufficient time, the present universe was bound to happen. But we do not know that. Since time itself appears to have begun in the Big Bang, the assumption of "sufficient time" isn't valid. (It's obviously meaningless to claim that, given a long enough stretch of time, time was bound to come into existence.) The initial conditions could just as easily—and probably more easily—have *prevented* the existence of the cosmos. Odd as it sounds, a big topic for scientists is why there is anything, as opposed to nothing! The mind-bending arguments may be difficult to follow. At least we should know the bottom line: Science has determined that the world has not always been here.

"Who made God?"

The skeptic may gibe, "Who created the Creator?" Yet by definition God is uncreated; he has always existed. Only those things that come into existence require a cause. But Yahweh is uncaused; he always was. He is spirit (John 4:24)—not composed of atoms or subatomic particles or photons. Yahweh isn't part of the physical world, and in some sense stands outside it. (He is the "I Am.") Yet just because he's outside the scope of scientific investigation doesn't mean he isn't real, since much of the real world is non-physical (truth, justice, beauty, love, numbers, etc.).

The Kalam Cosmological Argument

When discussing questions of creation, you might find help from the Kalam Cosmological Argument (KCA), for which the credit goes to medieval Islam. It is also supported by the laws of thermodynamics (the conservation of mass and energy).

The Kalam Cosmological Argument goes like this:

1. Whatever begins to exist has a cause.
2. The universe began to exist.
3. Therefore, the universe has a cause.

This form of the Kalam argument doesn't tell us what that cause was, yet for most of us the conclusion is obvious. In brief, the universe, which has existed only a few billion years, begs a Creator. God, who—unlike the universe—has always existed, is the best explanation. I am making a plausibility argument, not offering a rigorous scientific proof. Science cannot prove God, but the evidence suggests a God. As we see (and will continue to see in coming chapters), science is the friend of faith.

Points to Remember:

- Some atheists say God is unnecessary because the cosmos is infinitely old. We say God has always existed; they say the world has always existed; so we're even! But this counter won't work, since science has discovered that the universe had a beginning. It isn't infinitely old!
- There was nothing before the beginning—no matter, energy, space, or even time. The age of the universe thus strongly points in the direction of creation (a word many scientists use) and even a Creator.
- It's unnecessary to account for the origin of God, since he never came into being; he simply *is*, timeless and eternal.
- The mystery of the cosmos—where it came from, why it exists in the first place—is best approached with the insight that it was intentionally created.

CHAPTER 17

Does Science Contradict the Bible?

$\mathcal{S}$keptics frequently insist that science refutes the Bible, and that any intelligent, educated person must reject Scripture. What should we say in response? I often reply, "Do you know what believers mean when we refer to God's two Books?" I then explain that the Book of Words is Scripture, and the Book of Works is nature. (If this idea is new to you, persevere as I develop it—in the end, it'll be worth it!)

By "nature" we usually mean the natural world apart from human activity, though humans also occupy a niche in the natural world. Nature is more than sunrises and sunsets, walks in the forest, or documentaries on the wonders of our planet. Earth is but a minuscule part of the known world, and nature includes countless planets, stars, and galaxies. Astrophysicists enable us to peer at the boundaries of the universe, billions of light years away.

The psalmist affirmed, "The heavens declare the glory of God; the skies proclaim the work of his hands," and a few verses later, "The law of the LORD is perfect, reviving the soul. The statutes of the LORD are trustworthy, making wise the simple." (Ps 19:1,7). The first section of this beautiful hymn speaks of nature, the second of Scripture (and the third, our response to his revelation).

Yet a good many Christians suspect that God speaks to us only in the Bible. "Surely the Bible is our prayer book, history book, and science book. It tells us not just how we are to live, but also informs us on such matters as how old the world is." The principal problem with this view is that it runs up against passages like Ps 19:1, 8:1, and Rom 1:20, where the Bible affirms that God also speaks, at some level, in nature.

In fact there are even more ways in which the Lord speaks or has spoken (directly or indirectly): through the history of Israel, the person of Jesus Christ, our consciences, and through people who give us wise counsel.

Nature speaks

The subheading could be rephrased "What science demonstrates," as science is the systematic study of nature. Since God tells us that he reveals some truth in nature, we ought not to be conflicted or fearful that some discovery of science will overthrow Scripture. Rather, the thinking Christian welcomes the discoveries of science. Even if some theories may eventually be reworked or discarded, science on the whole is a noble venture and should be appreciated as a powerful ally for faith. "It is the glory of God to conceal things, but the glory of kings is to search things out" (Prov 25:2 ESV; see this principle illustrated in 1 Kgs 4:29–34).

Back in the early seventeenth century, the established church hesitated to accept the truth that the earth orbits the sun, since the Scriptures state, "[The world] shall never be moved" (Ps 93:1 ESV). Yet as the evidence piled up, the priests gave in, eventually accepting Galileo's position—even though they had held him under house arrest for publishing this very truth! Yet this was an unnecessary battle—and a foolish one—in the first place. The Bible is not a science book, and any passages that touch on science or the workings of nature were not presented as central doctrine—they were incidental. Often, they were idiomatic or metaphorical. For example, ancient writers used idioms that would make sense to readers of their day. Just as a modern writer might say, "The sun rises in the east" (knowing that in fact the sun does not rise; rather, the earth rotates), so Bible writers also used idioms that would be widely understood by their readers (Gen 19:23; Eccl 1:5). Or when the psalmist writes, "In the heavens God has pitched a tent for the sun. . . . . [The sun] rises at one end of the heavens and makes its circuit to the other; nothing is deprived of its warmth" (Ps 19:4, 6), he is indulging in both metaphoric and hyperbolic language for the sake of poetry. The Bible isn't a science book, any more than a biology text is intended to strengthen our relationship with God! The Book of Nature and the Book of Words address different aspects of reality.

Implications

What are the implications of the doctrine of the two Books? There are several, and they are important:

- **God does not deceive us, even through nature.** I have met Christians who reject the existence of dinosaurs, simply because dinosaurs aren't mentioned in Scripture. When I ask about the fossils, they say, "God allowed the devil to put those bones in the ground to harden the hearts of the incorrigible." But such a deception is not in line with the character of the biblical God!

- **God's two Books are complementary, not contradictory.** Most "contradictions" between the Bible and science easily disappear once the nature and intention of each Book are understood. The two Books complement one another, but that doesn't mean that the Bible supplies some scientific knowledge and the scientists add further data. It means that the subject matter of each Book is different, and helps us to understand different aspects of God. The Bible is a book of relationships, justice, and mercy. It shows us the tender heart of God. Science is a "book" of empirical study. It shows us the majesty, wisdom, and power of God.

- **The universe is probably as old as it appears.** Some people plead the *omphalos* hypothesis. *Omphalos* is the Greek word for belly button. Did Adam have a navel? If so, they reason, Adam was created with an appearance of age, whereas in fact he was only seconds old. So, they say, it is with the world: scientific study indicates the earth is billions of years old, but it's actually only six thousand years old, and they claim they have scientific evidence to bolster their young-earth views. Yet their reasoning fails for two reasons. First, even if there is scientific evidence that the earth is young, then by reason of *omphalos* we would never know it, since the earth *appears* to be old. Second, and more important, the *omphalos* hypothesis makes God a deceiver, whereas Satan is the one who is the deceiver (Rev 12:9).

Conceit or laziness?

Let's ask ourselves: What kind of an attitude do I have towards learning God's truth? Do I value the Book of Words but not the Book of Works? Or vice versa? Do I pit Scripture against nature, finding "contradictions" where there are none? Have I bought into any shallow arguments that make me feel better about not working to get at the facts? In his 1605 book *The Advancement of Learning*, Francis Bacon (1561–1626), "the Father of Empiricism," gave us a well-worded challenge (I wish I'd written this!):

> "Let no man or woman, out of conceit or laziness, think or believe that anyone can search too far or be too well informed in the Book of God's Words or in the Book of God's Works: Religion or Science. Instead, let everyone endlessly improve their understanding of both."[16]

Points to Remember:

- **Revelation:** God reveals truth in two books, the Book of Words (Scripture) and the Book of Works (nature). It's only with both Books that we learn to appreciate the full grandeur of God's revelation. Exalting science above Scripture isn't the way to seek all of God's truth, nor should we ignore the results of science in the name of faith.
- **Confidence:** Since God speaks truth, and he has told us that part of this truth is revealed in nature (Ps 19), we can have a high level of confidence in the discoveries of science. Yahweh will not deceive us.

- **Controversy:** Several of the church's historical blunders have issued from a failure to discern the two Books. (Dragons, a flat earth, dinosaurs living with humans, a six-thousand-year-old universe, and Galileo's trials all come to mind as examples.) Criticisms of modern science that spring from supposed contradictions with the Bible are often poorly constructed and easily dismantled, and they drive many thinkers away from Christianity.

- **Harmony:** The two Books are complementary, not contradictory. A broadly educated Christian will make efforts not only to be a man or woman of the word, but also a student of the world.

CHAPTER 18

Intelligent Design

G od's world everywhere shows unmistakable evidence of design:

- The cosmos appears to be "fine-tuned": dozens of parameters seem to have been taken into account and most of the variables adjusted with nearly infinitesimal accuracy to produce a life-sustaining universe that could give rise to science itself. For example, if someone tweaked the gravitational constant, or the ratio of the mass of a proton to that of a neutron, or the ratio of matter to antimatter, by *even one percent,* there would be no life in the universe. Planets would fail to form, or stellar nuclei would never produce the heavier elements needed for life in a stable environment.

- Further, we may observe the principle of mathematical elegance: natural laws and processes expressed in concise mathematical formulae. The laws of nature allow us to predict, to extrapolate. Without them, there would be no real science. This makes sense when we consider that the founders of modern science were nearly all believers in a deity. They expected the world to be rational, since it was created by a God of reason.

- The argument from design (*teleology*, if you prefer the term philosophers and theologians use) is simple. The cosmos is either purposive or not. (If you want the platinum term, a world without purpose and God is *dysteleological*.) Since the universe appears designed to lead to human life (what is called the "anthropic principle"), and humans are in turn able to observe and utilize the laws of nature, the assumption that there is a God is at least as rational as the assumption that there isn't.

A skeptic might counter, "Yes, I concede, the world of quarks and atoms, quasars and nebulae, intelligence and personality, does look as though it's been designed by a divinity. But since the universe has been here forever, it was only a matter of time before such a cosmos appeared. And even if it didn't, there may be infinite universes, so sooner or later a world like our own was bound to come along. We don't need to bring in God to explain the world." Several thoughts strike me immediately:

- Since the world hasn't been here forever (infinite time), but only billions of years, the confidence that such a world would occur are still remote. Some mathematicians calculate the odds of such a world coming into existence without God are poorer than 1 in 10^{124}. (The total number of subatomic particles estimated to exist in the universe is 1 in 10^{80}.)[17]
- Since matter itself came into being, removing God gives no advantage to the skeptic, since he still has to account for why there's anything in the first place.
- It seems more reasonable that a universe displaying signs of intelligence (design) and personality (consider human life) has its origin in a power that is both intelligent and personal.
- There is no empirical proof of a multiverse. The theory is speculative. And even if there were a parallel universe (or something like that), unless it somehow intersected our own (the kind of thing parallel lines are indisposed to do) we would still be in the dark. Proposing a multiverse isn't the same as proving

it. But even if there were a multiverse, the same questions about origins beg explanation. If we believe one universe requires an explanation like God, how about a million worlds, or an infinite number? The need for God would be all the greater!

- While design is highly suggestive of intelligence and purpose, it doesn't prove (scientifically) that there is a God. Nevertheless, it makes the theist's position plausible—more plausible than the atheist's.

"Intelligent Design"?

Does the abundant evidence of intelligence in the world's design require us to believe in the theory of "Intelligent Design" (ID)? This view, popular since the 1990s, is ambivalent towards modern biology, for it rules out the most impressive processes, unwilling to attribute them to natural causes. ID claims a miracle whenever science hasn't quite caught up with observation. For example, ID only partially accepts evolution. It has a history of taking complicated processes for which we have significant scientific evidence, and explaining them away with vague, over-simplified, and unsatisfying conclusions that essentially amount to, "This development is a miracle performed by an intelligent designer." In my view, it fails to honor the principle of the two Books (God's handiwork revealed through the natural world and in his written word), and promotes skepticism.

Yet ID accepts the scientific evidence for the enormous antiquity of the world (billions of years). It allows microevolution. But when there's a gap in scientific knowledge, watch out: ID inserts a miracle to bridge the distance. The problem is, as the gaps are filled—science explaining more and more—the frontier retreats, and the proper sense of mystery is (unnecessarily) lost.

ID affirms God as Creator, but it underestimates the creative power of the natural processes God has facilitated in his world. It puts the two Books in a state of conflict, when in fact they are not. ID's picture of a "God of the Gaps" is rightly rejected by atheists. Agreeing (as I do) that the universe displays both intelligence and design is not the same as accepting ID.

Three possibilities

Given the stunningly complex nature of the physical world, not to mention the many intangible realities we all experience (love, beauty, truth, and so on), is there a satisfactory theory to account for what we observe? There are only three possibilities.

- **The universe didn't come into being; it just always was.** So believe many unbelievers. Yet science has shown that the universe *has* come into being. The universe had a beginning! Moreover, scientific laws require that whatever comes into being must have a cause.

That means only two options remain:
- **The universe is self-caused**. This isn't much better than the first idea. How did nothing become something (during the Big Bang)? If there was nothing there, how did the universe "bang" itself into existence?

As self-causation fails to persuade, we are left with only one conclusion:
- **The universe was caused by something external to itself.** This can't be something physical, since that would in turn require its own cause, ad infinitum. The ultimate cause must lie outside the universe. What could be capable of creating the vast cosmos we observe, with its overwhelming complexity, order, beauty, and design—including human life? Surely God is the best explanation.

Proof, or suggestion?

Our conclusion is not that the impression of design *proves* there's a designer; it is more modest. We argue only that design *suggests* a designer. The gentler phrasing of our reasoning may, in the long term, convince more people than will be won by grandiose claims. Perhaps this reasoning will plant a seed in a thinking person that one day might germinate into faith.

Points to Remember:

- God's world shows unmistakable traces of design. Natural processes follow rational laws—laws anticipated by scientists whose strength was their confidence in a God of reason. Thus the argument (for God's existence) from design moves from design to designer.
- While design is highly *suggestive* of intelligence and purpose, it doesn't *prove* God. Nevertheless, it makes the theist's position more plausible than the atheist's. We should not hesitate to point this out.
- "Intelligent Design" is on track in attributing intelligence and design to an intelligent designer. The universe's stunning levels of complexity indicate a God. Yet we don't need to posit a miracle (as ID does) every time an unbelievably intricate biological structure develops. God is able to work his will through a lengthy process just as easily as through immediate creation.
- As for the origins of the world (cosmology), there are but three possibilities: the cosmos is uncaused, self-caused, or externally caused. Science refutes the first two, so we're left with the third: something or someone *outside* caused the universe to come into being. Considering not only the vastness of the cosmos but also its design features (complexity, order, beauty, function, mathematical precision), the best explanation is God.

CHAPTER 19

Can a Christian Believe in Evolution?

One day I was walking the streets of London, sharing my faith in Christ, when I was invited to a service in progress. I agreed to join. The group was small, and their central doctrine was that the theory of evolution is Satanic, and lies behind all the ills of our modern world. If you accept evolution, you cannot be saved, but if you renounce evolution, then you can be a true Christian. The group welcomed me until they discovered that I didn't agree evolution was a salvation issue. Their dogma may not have been flexible, but their church service was, and for the next hour the chairs were rearranged so that everyone faced me. I was grilled by their pastor in a special "Convert Douglas" session. Alas, I remained an infidel, refusing to give up my faith in the Bible and science.

This may serve to remind us that for many people, evolution is a sensitive subject. For others it is only intriguing, awakening a sense of wonder. And yet for a significant number of people, evolution is a decisive issue, determining your salvation.

Evolution is sensitive because many (mainly inside the borders of the US) equate modern biology with rejection of the Bible. For them, acceptance or rejection of evolution is a shibboleth indicating whether someone is a true believer. In the county where I live (in Georgia), pressure from parent groups once forced the placement of stickers in local schools' science textbooks that said, "Evolution is theory, not fact."

These stickers were likely inserted by well-meaning believers who thought that you could not believe in both God and evolution. But this position forces a false distinction and unnecessary division. Just as the people who feared the Big Bang theory would overturn their faith were wrong—the Big Bang theory strongly supports faith!—so it is with biology. We have nothing to fear from biology, and especially from evolutionary ideas. Studying the origin and diversification of life is nothing short of stunning. It should build our faith, not threaten it. Evolution itself provides strong support for theism.

The study of evolution is intriguing because the level of detail we find in nature is fascinating, and the science that reveals the dynamics of life is cutting edge. As we grow in our understanding and respect for God's Book of Works, we can be blown away by his wonders in the biological world! The experience is not unlike worship. Some people have come to faith *because of* evolution, overwhelmed by its elegance. One eminent example is Francis Collins, possibly the most recognizable scientist in the U.S. today, especially since his team at the National Institutes of Health successfully sequenced the entire human genome. *The Language of God* (Free Press, 2006) is his bestselling story of how evolution brought him to faith in the God of the Bible, and it is well worth reading.

And evolution is a decisive issue because many Christians leave God when forced to choose between what they learned in Sunday School and what they're learning in bio class. Similarly, far too many seekers are driven away by the anti-science stance of some churches. When presented with a choice ("It's evolution or God—pick one!"), it's hardly a surprise that many people, now better informed about the science, are conflicted.

Disputable matters

In this chapter we're not going to weigh the evidence for or against evolution. (We will touch on some of that in the next chapter.) The point of this chapter is to emphasize that we should resist a false choice, especially when it's connected with false consequences ("You'll go to hell if you endorse Darwin").

Evolution is *not* a matter of salvation. Most Christians would agree that it's a "disputable matter" (Rom 14:1). As with other issues, the truth baldly stated could cause a "weaker" brother to stumble, and so it is incumbent on those who are better informed to be sensitive to those who are not. Paul wrote, "Let us not pass judgment on one another any longer, but rather decide never to put a stumbling block or hindrance in the way of a brother. . . . Do not let what you regard as good be spoken of as evil. . . . Let us pursue what makes for peace and for mutual upbuilding" (Rom 14:13–19 ESV).

The two camps: creationists vs. evolutionists

The father of contemporary Young Earth creationism was Henry M. Morris (1918–2006), who stated, "There are only two basic world views . . . creation or evolution."[18] Despite the scientific evidence for the age of the earth, he claimed, "There is no evidence that the world is old." Morris's opinion brooked no compromise: "Satan himself is the originator of the concept of evolution."[19] (I once wrote to Morris, and to his credit he replied personally, although he didn't answer my questions—instead he enclosed a stack of pamphlets I'd already read.)

Exemplary of the other side, the late Christopher Hitchens (1949–2011) wrote: "Now at last you can be properly humble in the face of your maker, which turns out not to be a 'who,' but a process of mutation with rather more random elements than our vanity might wish."[20] Yet as an evolutionist, Hitchens reached way past Darwin in his conclusions. *The Origin of Species* admits there is a God. Even twenty years after he published his groundbreaking book, Darwin wrote in a private letter, "It seems to me absurd to doubt that a man may be an ardent Theist and an evolutionist."[21]

For Darwin, who was more agnostic than atheist—he continued to wrestle with faith issues throughout his life, and continued to support foreign missions—there was no need to choose between his theory and the Almighty. Most of Darwin's early supporters were churchmen, in both England and in the United States—thinking persons who understood the *why* of life on earth, but looked to science (God's Book of Works) for the *how*. Things soon became polarized; within a few decades evolution became a highly charged issue.

I considered myself a Young Earth creationist from age sixteen to twenty, then an Old Earth creationist (the earth is billions of years old—just as old as it appears to be—yet God assisted the natural processes of evolution with the occasional miracle). By 2005 I had become an evolutionary creationist (holding a high degree of trust in both science and the Bible). I've read enough books on the topic (nearly 100) and attended enough conferences to know how passionately people can feel about this issue. When I present on science, I strive to be fair with the facts, while also taking a broad look at the history of the Christian church, which has often found itself on the wrong side of science. In my evolution debate with *Scientific American*'s Michael Shermer (we've now debated each other three times), I refused to choose between science and faith, and I believe everyone should refuse to be coerced into a false choice.

Must we choose?

Perhaps you are reaching out to someone who is still wrestling with how faith interacts with science, particularly with evolution. While continually weighing the issues, they're striving for intellectual integrity. We're on the same side! They may accept the evidence that the world is ancient, most species have gone extinct, and the biological world is in constant flux. You can help them understand that Genesis 1 was written to tell us of the wisdom and orderliness of the Creator, not to be used as a timeline. Encourage your friend that they need not be pressed up against a wall or declare a position too quickly. They don't have to choose between evolution and the Bible. They can believe in both! They should take time to carefully weigh the evidence, confident that God's Book of Works will not mislead us any more than will his Book of Words.

Many noted believers refuse to be drawn into the fray, whatever their leaning. I appreciate the perspective of evangelist Billy Graham: "I believe that God did create the universe. I believe that God created man, and whether it came by an evolutionary process and at a certain point he took this person or being and made him a living soul or not, does not change the fact that God did create man . . . whichever way

God did it makes no difference as to what man is and man's relationship to God."[22] If Graham and others are right, evolution should be a non-issue. It should not be used as a test of fellowship. And we ought to conduct ourselves respectfully towards those who may disagree with our conclusions.

The church or science: Choose now!

For centuries the church taught that the sun orbited the earth. There seemed to be abundant biblical ammunition to defend the geocentric model while blasting all alternative views out of the water. For example, the Bible says, "The sun rises and the sun sets, and hurries back to where it rises" (Eccl 1:5). Is this true or not? What would you say to someone who demanded that you choose between the sun rising and the scientifically correct "earth rising"? Is it worth fighting over? Probably not—but in the 1500s this was a hot issue. Copernicus had to keep his view under wraps, and in the 1600s Galileo endured censorship and house arrest, even after proving the old geocentric model was hopelessly flawed. Might this be a parallel to the current uproar over evolution?

Appealing or appalling?

I realize that some of my readers are thrilled that I'm addressing the findings of modern biology, while others are probably appalled. Please bear with me, and read all the way through the chapters I offer on the topic before making up your mind. In the next two chapters we'll examine several aspects of evolutionary biology, addressing the most common objections to evolution and offering some suggestions on how to respond to someone who's using evolution as an excuse not to believe in God or the Bible.

In the meantime, keep in mind that the enemy isn't evolution, but *atheistic* evolution. The first is neutral with respect to God; the other is anti-God, and should be rejected. Further, it's a mistake to judge someone's salvation on the basis of scientific knowledge; we're saved by faith, not by knowledge. It's one thing if someone rejects God—clearly he is not my brother in Christ. Yet it's quite another if he's only rejecting my interpretation of Genesis. In that case, there's ample room for fellowship, even if we disagree, and we will do well to remember Paul's advice in Romans 14.

Here are a few points to consider:

- **The how vs. the why:** Science deals with the *how*: natural processes, developmental stages, chemical reactions, and so on. Scripture deals more with the *why*: God's reason for creation, his ultimate will for us, etc. As long as we distinguish the how from the why, we're unlikely to find contradictions between nature and Scripture.

- **Category error:** The Bible is not meant to be trawled for scientific principles. Although the scientific evidence is virtually unassailable, partially informed understandings of evolution have muddied the water. Some believers attempt to read Scripture as a scientific document. Yet the Bible is a book of relationships, not biology, chemistry, or physics. Genesis, as part of God's Book of Words, tells of us of true spiritual origin: a loving God. For our physical origins, we may consult his Book of Works, nature—which is apprehended through science.

- **Being considerate:** Since for some believers evolution is a "disputable matter," people with strong opinions should bend over backwards to be considerate of those who might stumble (Rom 14). As long as one believes God is the Creator, he or she is on track biblically. One's scientific understanding of creation is not a salvation matter.

- **Geocentrism:** A rough parallel to the controversy over evolution during the last half-century in the US was the disagreement (around the year 1600) over the motion of the earth. The Bible repeatedly affirms that the earth can never be moved, and that the sun rises and sets. Yet science presents a different view. Does God want us to take Eccl 1:5 literally? Over time, Christians came to accept the fact that astro-gymnastics would be required to preserve the old geocentric model.

Let us learn to "read" science and the Bible in the manner which God intended, and let us resist making an unnecessary choice. To embrace pseudoscience, or to reject the Bible as uninspired (mistaken science)—neither choice is necessary. The God of truth is the God of *all* truth, whether found in the Bible or in the laboratory.

Points to Remember:

- Science deals with the *how* of creation; Scripture addresses the *why*.
- The current controversy over evolution is reminiscent of the conflict over geocentrism in the 1600s.
- There is room for diversity in believers' opinions about evolution and science. We should be respectful of others' views, and careful about airing our own too aggressively.
- It is unnecessary to choose between creation and evolution, God and science.

CHAPTER 20

Genesis, Creation, and Evolution

Scientific Responses to "Christian" Objections

n ature and Scripture, as we have seen, are complementary. This means that science and theology should be complementary, too. Might science and Genesis clash less than we think? Could God have used the process of evolution for the creation and diversification of life forms?

In this chapter we will address the common objections some *Christians* have made about science, Darwin, evolution, and the creation story as they read it in Genesis.

1. "Evolution is only a theory, not fact."

I used to say this myself! But to be fair, that's not how the word *theory* is used in science. A theory is a comprehensive explanation of the facts, a way of making sense of the data. Gravitation is a theory, yet that hardly means we would be safe skydiving without a parachute. Einstein forever changed how gravity is understood, but he didn't render gravity obsolete. At any rate, evolution is well supported by facts: the fossil record, speciation even today, and the conclusive findings of genetics. It is possible that a better theory, or a different version of the theory, will one day undermine our current understanding of evolution. Evolution isn't sacrosanct, just the best model for what is observed.

2. "No true Christian accepts evolution."

Actually, nearly all accept at least some evolution; the disagreement lies in how much. Microevolution, the accumulation of small changes through reproduction, is hardly controversial. Some Christians deny macroevolution (one species changing into another), while others accept most (but not all) macroevolutionary events. And it is normal for believers working in science to accept evolution as a robust working hypothesis. The only view we men and women of faith are bound to reject is *atheistic* evolution—the mistaken notion that even without God there would be a creation.

3. "Darwin undermines faith."

As noted last week, Charles Darwin had no intention of rendering faith obsolete. He was only trying to make sense of the facts. When Darwin released his book *On the Origin of Species* (1859), some of his biggest fans were Bible believers! Already before 1800 the entire geological column, with its unvarying succession of levels and fossils, had been worked out, with the implication that the world was unspeakably ancient. The conclusion had been reached not by skeptics, but by Bible believers.

4. "Scientists unfairly rule out the supernatural."

Science deals with nature, not supernature. It's neither for nor against the supernatural. A Geiger counter has no bias against kilograms; it just can't weigh them. Similarly, neither is science prejudiced against the beauty of a symphony. It has nothing to say about beauty, even if it can explain the acoustics of sound. A few scientists have an agenda, and trade on their authority in one (fairly small) domain to lecture others on faith, though in my experience most scientists are persons of integrity.

5. "If evolution is true, then we're only animals! Your great-great-great- grandfather may have been an ape, but mine wasn't. The notion is insulting."

The Bible classifies us as both *belonging to* and *ruling over* the animals—but only when we live spiritually, faithfully bearing the image of God. Otherwise, we begin to descend to the level of the flesh. Genetically we have much in common with other animals. Yet, unlike them, we have a choice: to live by the flesh or to live by the Spirit! For the person insulted by human evolution, it gets worse. The Bible describes us as made of earth (Gen 2:7). Dirt! Adam, which is a play on words with 'adamah (the word for earth, ground, dust) reminds us of our lowly origins and our heavenly Creator. Remembering our origins should keep us humble!

6. "Scientists disagree over evolution."

It is true that some scientists outside the field of biology qualify their acceptance of evolution, but for those who work in such areas as genetics, molecular biology, botany and zoology, the theory is a given. More than ninety-nine percent of scientists accept it! This is not to say that most scientists look to the theory for meaning; the majority of scientists in our world are believers, standing in awe of God's ways, and are usually careful about worshiping only the Creator, not his creation.

7. "There are only two interpretations of the facts: biblical creation a few thousand years ago, or atheistic evolution."

Actually, just as evolutionists have differing perspectives, there are a variety of positions among believers: Young Earth creationism, Old Earth creationism, deism, and evolutionary creationism.[23] Again, every creationist I've met accepts evolution. The question is, how much?

8. "Fiat creation must be instantaneous, unlike evolution."

Their reasoning goes something like this: "*Bara'* is Hebrew for *ex nihilo* (out of nothing) creation, in contrast with '*asah,* meaning *to shape* (to make or form from something preexisting). *Bara',* not '*asah,* is used in Genesis 1." This argument doesn't work. First, Genesis uses *bara'* in both senses, and the words are nearly synonyms. *Bara'* is the verb used in Isaiah 44:21, where God *creates* Israel. Yet she came to be a people through a process spanning centuries, with many twists and turns along the way. The notion that it is beneath God to act slowly is flawed. His normal way of working is through processes. Consider pregnancy, forestation, and spiritual formation: nothing is instantaneous. That just isn't the way he works. The question isn't what God *could* have done; it's what the evidence indicates.

9. "Genesis 1 depicts God creating all kinds directly."

Genesis 1:11 and v. 24 say otherwise ("Let the land produce vegetation. . . . Let the land produce living creatures"), so if you want to take this language literally, we have the land somehow producing both plants and animals. Indirect creation makes more sense than direct.

10. "The Bible says God created the world in seven twenty-four-hour days."

Genesis 1 contains one of five or six creation stories in the Bible. In Gen 1, creation is portrayed as taking place in a week, probably to emphasize the importance of Sabbath for the Jews. This account is semi-poetic. Historically speaking, most Jews and Christians during the last two or three millennia have *not* taken this literally. There are five major interpretations in all. With only a little spadework, you can know which makes the best sense to you.

11. "Well, the order in Genesis 1 is the same as what we see in the fossil record."

Not really. Even if we table the question of the creation of sun and moon (day 4), the fossil record shows animals as preceding plants, not plants preceding animals (as in day 3). Science has discovered that life almost certainly originated in the oceans, not on land (as on day 3). So the biblical order doesn't match the fossil record at all. That's probably because in the Genesis account, creation has been placed in its true position, not as gods to be worshiped (the contemporary sun god has been demoted to a "big light"). Days 1, 2, and 3 are the Lord's provision of the right environments for the creations of days 4, 5, and 6, respectively.

12. "Evolution is nothing other than 'spontaneous generation,' an ancient view disproved two centuries ago."

But in evolution, life doesn't come from nothing; there are preexisting ingredients, and after the first unicellular animal in the primeval ocean, it was only a matter of the descendants of one life form transforming into others.

13. "We can't trust the fossil evidence, since sometimes things are backwards, or the expected layers have disappeared completely."

In fact, the sequences are invariable, although occasionally some layers are destroyed by erosion (with the land heaving and subsiding, to be exposed to water) or overturned through colossal natural forces (like volcanic eruption).

14. "Mutations are harmful, and could never lead to any significant improvement—much less to the development of new structures or species."

Yet the harmful mutations are weeded out as the life forms affected by them lose out in the struggle to pass on genes. The accumulation of mutations that bring a survival advantage has been shown to lead to new structures and even new species. New species are continually developing on the planet. *Scientific American*, *Nature*, and other journals can guide us through the new discoveries.

15. "The earth is way too young for evolution to have happened."

Not so. Evolution is happening now, with new species (not just subspecies) observed every year. There are dozens of accurate dating techniques, and all suggest a world enormously older than any estimate the Young Earth movement has ever suggested. On the other hand, unless God had set the initial conditions ("fine-tuning for life"), the chance of our world coming into existence would have been infinitesimal. If the atheists are right, the world is way too young to have gotten so lucky.

16. "Evolution violates the Second Law of Thermodynamics."

This law, regarding thermodynamic systems, holds that total entropy (the tendency of a system to move to disorganization) is conserved, or even increases. While this is true for a closed system, the earth is *not* a closed system. It continuously receives inputs of energy (like sunlight) and mass (like meteors), which feed and drive a number of processes (like photosynthesis).

17. "Hitler appealed to evolution to justify inhuman ideas and actions."

The Crusaders appealed to the Bible, too, but their misuse and wicked applications don't nullify Scripture. Nazism was (and is) horrible, and there's no doubt its engineers misused science to further their ends. However, even though the objection carries a lot of emotional freight, it isn't relevant to the discussion of whether evolution is true.

18. "The Bible doesn't mention the Big Bang or evolution, so they can't be true."

The Bible doesn't mention dinosaurs, galaxies, or Australia either, but that hardly means we should reject the fossils, insult the astronomers, or doubt there's a land "Down Under." In fact, *most* of the objects and events in the history of the universe pass without comment in Scripture. Remember, the Bible focuses on relationships. It has little, if any, interest in science.

19. "Evolution is a slippery slope."

Many people fear that if they accept evolution, they're opening the door to atheism. This need not be so. Consider the literature of the Bible. Roughly one third of Scripture is poetic. Does acknowledging that somehow lead to rejecting the historical facts of the Bible? Can't people tell the difference? The earth is described as resting atop pillars (Job 9:6, 26:11; Ps 75:3), yet surely this is the ancient concept, incidental and not a matter of doctrine. Without distinguishing ancient conceptions from modern science, we end up in a tangle.

Or take communion wine. Despite the biblical evidence that it was alcoholic, many churches fear the use of wine could plunge their members into alcoholism and drug addiction. That may be so, but it doesn't mean we should ignore the facts that call our theory into question. The slope becomes slippery only when morals and faith are incorrectly linked with the rejection of a neutral theory (evolution).

Thus we see that Christians' common objections to evolution are easily answered. Please remember, wherever you land on these matters, this isn't a salvation issue. When it's incorrectly viewed in that way, then we have forgotten the important message of 1 Cor 4:6: "Do not go beyond what is written."

Points to Remember:

Since this chapter has 19 points, here we will restate only a few.

- A scientific *theory* (like the theory of evolution or the theory of gravity) is a robust explanation making sense of the data. Since "theory" does not mean "guess," calling evolution "only a theory" is misleading.
- By 1800 the entire geological column, with its unvarying succession of levels and fossils, had been worked out, with the implication that the world was unspeakably ancient. The conclusion had been reached not by skeptics, but by Bible believers. And Darwin's early fans included many Christians— at long last there was an explanation for what they'd observed.
- Contrary to common claims, Gen 1 *doesn't* depict God creating all kinds directly (see 1:11 and 1:24). Nor does Gen 1 present creation in the order found in God's Book of Works, nature (nature indicates that animals preceded plants). Nor is the scientific explanation hopelessly at odds with the lofty, divine depiction of the creation of humans in Gen 1, since the Bible also says we are made of dirt (Gen 2:7). Finally, fiat creation need not be instantaneous, as illustrated in Isa 44:21, where God *creates* Israel through a process spanning centuries. The notion that it is beneath God to act slowly is flawed.
- The fact that Hitler and others appealed to evolution to justify inhuman choices is irrelevant to whether evolution is true.

Nor does the "slippery slope" argument hold water. The slope becomes slippery only when people have been told that if evolution is true, there's no God.

CHAPTER 21

Genesis, Creation, and Evolution
Christian Responses to Skeptic Objections

*I*n the last chapter, we answered some Christians' concerns about how evolution and science relate to faith and the Bible. In this chapter, we'll look at the same topics from the *skeptic's* perspective. Many non-believers hold misconceptions about what the Bible says about creation and science. (Surely the confusion and ambivalence within the Christian community have not helped their impression!) Let's take four prevalent objections a skeptic might have about Genesis, the creation story, and evolution, and suggest responses the believer might make in return.

1. "In portraying a six-day creation six thousand years ago, Genesis is hopelessly confused."

The Bible doesn't say how old the world is, or commit us to a single creation account. The six-thousand-year notion is only an interpretation—an incorrect one—foisted onto the biblical material. Further, the Bible presents creation in different ways through multiple images (e.g. Gen 1:1–2:4a; Gen 2:4b–22; Ps 89:9–11; Prov 8:22–31). Genesis 1 utilizes a sabbatical framework. The point is the Lord's providence: he provided environments in days 1, 2, and 3; he brought forth the creations that would inhabit them in days 4, 5, and 6, respectively. Humans are the crowning creation, and then comes the Sabbath. Such a portrayal, rejecting the creation myths of contemporary peoples, was written to keep God's people faithful—especially as they were in exile in Babylon. Genesis tells us about God. It does so in terms intelligible to the people living in the time in which it was written. (That's why it describes a solid dome—a "firmament"—over a flat and circular earth, sun and stars circling the earth, floodgates in heaven, and so on.)

Just as a first-grade teacher simplifies and accommodates a lesson so that six-year-olds will understand, so the Lord spoke to humans in terms they could understand. As in the incarnation, in the Bible he comes down to our level. Like the incarnate Word, the written word aims for intelligibility more than technical knowledge. Statements that *could* be viewed as scientific (we considered Eccl 1:5 in an earlier chapter) are usually incidental. The Bible makes no scientific affirmations, but many theological ones.

2. "Countless eons to create stars and planets and life, and millions of species already extinct! Why the waste?"

The Lord apparently isn't in a rush. It takes billions of years for the heavier elements to be formed in the nuclei of stars. Life on earth has a long history, both flora and fauna. Consider the ancient forests: much of the wood material was buried and subjected to intense geologic pressure, and converted over time into fossil fuels. (We have benefitted from those energy sources!) Nothing is wasted. When we survey the natural world, or even the human world, we observe that the Lord's normal way of working is through processes. Take, for example, pregnancy, glaciation, and character formation. All require time—lots of it!

3. "I've been told I can't accept the Big Bang and evolution and still be a Christian. When Christians try to convince me, they get the science all wrong. I'm not sure I want to follow a God who's opposed to rational thought."

I'm sorry—your experience is really unfortunate. You've been confronted with a false choice. Sixteen hundred years ago a brilliant

Christian was embarrassed when his fellow believers spoke in ignorance, muddying the water, so to speak. Augustine (354–430) wrote, "Usually, a Christian knows something about the natural world. Now, it is a disgraceful and dangerous thing for an unbeliever to hear a Christian, presumably giving the meaning of Holy Scripture, talking nonsense on these topics. The danger is not so much that the individual is made fun of, as that outsiders suppose that the writers of the Bible held these opinions. If they find a Christian mistaken in a field which they themselves know well and hear him maintaining his foolish opinions about our books, how are they going to believe the significantly more important doctrines of the Bible?"[24] So I guess I'd say, listen to your Christian friends when they are explaining the gospel, but filter out the extraneous comments when they're off topic.

4. "If Christianity is true, then why is science at odds with the Bible?"
Science is *not* at odds with Scripture (although some scientists may oppose the beliefs of some preachers). Most scientists don't know Scripture, and haven't studied theology. And most preachers aren't professional scientists. The two groups can therefore easily talk past one another, especially when politics comes into play. I have met two world-class academics who are exceptions to this pattern. John Polkinghorne (theoretical physicist and theologian) is one. The other is my friend Denis Lamoureux, who holds three doctorates, including one in biology and one in theology. These men see no contradiction between Scripture and science—as long as the Scriptures are read correctly, and science doesn't overreach into philosophical or religious territory.

Putting it all together
Science enables us to marvel at the creativity, power, wisdom, and providence of our God. Many passages direct us to God's Book of Works (Psalms 8, 19, 104; Rom 1; and more.) So science not only makes life easier to live; it also humbles us and motivates us to ask the big existential questions: What is the meaning of life? Who am I? How should I relate to others?

Yet science is neutral with respect to faith. You can't prove God by science. While some *scientists* might unfairly rule out the supernatural, *science* cannot do this. It can only measure the natural world, not the supernatural one. In the words of Austrian physicist and Nobel Prize winner Erwin Schrödinger (1887–1961), "[Science] puts all our experience in magnificently consistent order, but it is ghastly silent about all and sundry that is really near to our heart. . . . it knows nothing of beautiful or ugly, good or bad, God and eternity."[25]

Points to Remember:

- When a skeptic rejects Genesis as "unscientific," he's making the same mistake a Bible believer is making by appealing to Scripture for a scientific account. That's simply not the nature of Genesis or its primeval narrative.

- In communicating his word to us, the Lord simplifies explanations and focuses only to remove ignorance when there is a spiritual or relational consequence. Mentions of (for example) sunrise in Scripture are not erroneous or unscientific; they're simply incidental to the message.

- Since the Lord normally operates through processes, we shouldn't be surprised that the universe is as old as it is—even if humans only make their entry on the stage at 11:58 pm! Time with God is not the same as time with us.

- Science is not at odds with Scripture. Most scientists don't know Scripture, and haven't studied theology, just as most preachers aren't professional scientists. The two groups therefore easily talk past one another.

- Science can only measure the natural world, not the supernatural one. For the really good stuff, we need more than the Book of Works; we need God's Book of Words.

Part 6:
SUFFERING

In all my travels—whether to Europe or Africa, Asia or Latin America, or to various parts of the US—the most common and perhaps most important question I am asked is, "If there's a God, how come . . . (some terrible thing) . . . happened?" This is *the* classic question about good and evil, called "theodicy" (from the Greek words for *god* and *justice*). In this section we will look for biblical answers to difficult questions about suffering and pain.

CHAPTER 22

The Problem of Suffering

*O*ur world is full of pain: grief, angst and apprehension (emotional pain), loneliness (social pain), poverty (financial pain), and guilt (mental and spiritual pain). These typify the human condition. When someone asks, "Where was God when *that* happened?", "Why do bad things happen to good people?", or "If God is good, how come . . . ?" he or she is speaking from the heart. We want *someone* to be responsible. We want *somebody* to care. All of us—theists, atheists, agnostics—experience evil and suffering. Is it true that evil and undeserved suffering disprove God?

Here are seven key points Christians can make about suffering:

1. **No God, no morality.** Unless God exists, there is no morality to begin with, because God is the standard of goodness. If there is no God, then in the face of evil, no one can claim, "Hey—oppression is wrong!" All he can say is, "I don't like oppression," or "I wish people weren't oppressed." Morality and God are intimately connected, as we discussed in chapter 10, "Why Morality Means God."

2. **Some skeptics say, "If there's a God, he would have made my life pain-free."** How should we respond? No one can *know* that God's agenda (if he exists) is to eliminate the pain and suffering in our lives. Isn't it rather suspicious that we think we can discern God's agenda, and that it corresponds neatly with our own?

3. **Suffering often serves useful functions.** What sort of character would we have if life was a nonstop Disney World of pleasure (with the added bonus of free food and no lines)? Perseverance through suffering builds character (Rom 5:3–4). Both suffering and the sufferer are transformed. As Holocaust survivor Viktor Frankl put it, "Suffering ceases to be suffering in some way at the moment it finds meaning."[26] It is the believer who has suffered who has greatest credibility. As someone else said, "Never trust a Christian who doesn't walk with a limp." (I wish I'd said that!)

4. **We live in a moral universe, yet one in which good often goes unrewarded and evil unrequited in this life.** Justice demands a settling of accounts in the next life. Only by faith in God can we have assurance that the world isn't monstrously indifferent. The justice we claim to seek is inseparable from judgment day.

5. **God understands the pain of suffering, and not just because he is all-wise.** His understanding of suffering isn't only intellectual, but experiential, for once he walked this earth as one of us. Hebrews 2:18 encourages us, "Because he himself suffered when he was tempted, he is able to help those who are being tempted." In God's verbal message to us, the Scriptures, the theme of evil and suffering is ubiquitous. It disturbed Abraham and nonplussed Job; it was explained by the prophets, lamented in the Psalms, and clarified in the Apocalypse. Further, if even Jesus Christ had to drink the cup of suffering, why should we imagine we get a free pass?

6. **Free will is of the essence.** It's hard to imagine how God could be just in holding us accountable, or even how we could be truly human, in the absence of free will. Yet free will cannot mean only the option to do good, to live right, and to help

others. It must also mean the capacity to do evil, live badly, and hurt others—including the innocent.

7. **Christianity offers neither simplistic answers nor escape from pain.** The Scriptures are deeply nuanced on the topic of suffering. If true faith were an invitation to escape suffering, all the world would be lining up for baptism! The ever-popular "health and wealth gospel" promotes exactly this sort of misguided thinking. But authentic Christianity is an invitation to follow the One who died for us. It means bearing the cross, graciously bearing up under unjust suffering (and all other kinds of suffering).

Points to Remember:

- Without an external moral standard, who's to say something is evil? If there is no God, then there is (ultimately) no good or evil. Once again, without God, as the Marquis de Sade said, "whatever is, is right."
- A world with free will (a trait that defines humanity) entails the potential for sin and suffering.
- Christianity offers neither simplistic answers nor escape from pain.
- God himself has entered our world, meeting us in our pain in Jesus' life and death.

CHAPTER 23

Evil and Suffering

*A*s we explore the problem of suffering, we will cover three things.

1. First, a look at the origin of evil. We hesitate to allege that God created anything not "good" or "very good" (Gen 1), but if he created all that is, why shouldn't we consider him accountable? That's how many skeptics think.

2. Second, we'll examine three passages commonly used by believers to dismiss or soften the discussion of suffering and evil: Romans 8:28, Jeremiah 29:11–14, and 1 Chronicles 4:9–10 (all things for the good; hope and a future; the "prayer of Jabez"). All three are routinely taken out of context and pressed to support doctrines that aren't fully biblical.

3. Last, I'll suggest the *biblical* purpose of suffering. Warning: If you haven't considered this before, you may not like the answer. (I'm quite sure that many religious leaders find it distasteful.)

The Origin of Evil

A natural question occurring to all trying to wrap their heads around God's nature is this: Did God create evil? If he created everything that exists, it's difficult not to also credit him as the author of evil.

While God might be charged with creating evil indirectly, he cannot be charged with creating evil directly. Those (good) creatures who used their free will to reject the good were the true "creators" of evil. Before sin, evil was only *potential*, not *actual*; it didn't yet exist. In the beginning there was God (good), then a creation (very good), including creatures with free will (also good). Their sinful choices (bad) actualized or reified evil.

Yet evil isn't *real* in the way good is. Evil is an *absence* of good, as unrighteous actions *lack* virtue, or goodness. To illustrate, are heat and cold both real? They are not. The molecules in hot air are in rapid motion, causing warm air to rise. The molecules in cold air lack thermal energy, and so they are in low motion. (This also explains why no one pumps cold air into a balloon.) Understood this way, cold is nothing. It's the absence of heat. Similarly, evil is nothing but the absence of good.

Not all suffering is evil

Not all suffering is *morally* evil; some of it is "bad" in terms of being undesirable, unpleasant, or destructive.

God doesn't manage all events in the cosmos. This is true even of our lives. As Eccl 9:11 notes, "Time and chance happen to them all." The element of the random, which physicists and biologists understand is essential to life's existence and progress, occasionally leads to birth defects, cancer, or even hazardous weather often (unfairly) called "acts of God."

So when a skeptic asks why he should believe in a God who created evil, agree with him: "You shouldn't. But then God *didn't* create evil." Your friend may concede that most evil and suffering are the consequence of human decisions, but he's bound to ask, "What about tsunamis and volcanic eruptions and wildfires?" Suggest that natural disasters are part and parcel of our world, serving multiple essential functions. If our world weren't so "dangerous," there would be no life. Nor does God usually intervene by changing the laws of nature or insulating us from the consequences of our choices. Could God have created a different world, still conducive to human life, *without* natural disasters, without the potential of evil? Apparently not.

If we are to serve God wholeheartedly, we need to be confident in our knowledge that God is our loving Father, not a moral monster or the author of evil.

Three passages we'd better reconsider

Everyone quotes the Bible to support his or her position. Yet citing a passage doesn't provide biblical authority if the passage has been wrested from its context, or twisted into a shape the inspired author never intended. Let's reconsider three passages that are often taken out of context, misapplied, and misunderstood—even by well-meaning believers.

1. Romans 8:28 has been only partly understood

In Romans 8, Paul discussed suffering and persecution (vv.17–18, 35). When we experience pain or trouble, many Christians apply Rom 8:28 like a bandage over a cut. Our friends may aim to console us, saying, "It's all for the good," or "God has a plan." The appeal to Rom 8 is usually intended to make us feel better about the pain. We may hear that something really good will happen to outweigh our suffering, or that our financial losses will be reversed, or that God's ways are mysterious, his providence ever protecting us.

There's some truth in such comments, but what about the broader context? In Rom 8:29, God's intention is that we be conformed to the image of his Son. Imagine responding to suffering as Christ did! We might be misrepresented, abused, or physically exhausted. We might be in the crucible, under severe pressure. God's will is that we patiently endure, without bitterness. And how is that to happen? *Through the process of suffering*. In other words, rather than explaining away suffering, we ought to realize that things may well get worse before they get better (also a major theme in the book of Revelation). The problem is not so much that the passage has been twisted, as that it's been only partially understood.

2. Jeremiah 29:11–14 has been woefully misunderstood

When I first discovered Jeremiah 29:11–14, I was keen to use it to help believers to seek God. *"Hope and a future" is just what people want and need,* I thought. *How wonderful that God plans to prosper us—that life will be better if we put him first!* This is true, yet many readers today go well beyond the meaning of the passage, in belief that God has a personalized plan, specifically designed for the happiness of each believer. This is simply not true—or at least I've never found a scriptural passage that supports it. Rather, God's plan back in the sixth century BC was for his people to return from exile in Babylon, and that plan was to take seventy years (29:10). In other words, nearly all who heard Jeremiah's words would be dead before the plan was realized!

Many believers take Jer 29 to guarantee a quick blessing—part of our on-demand, drive-thru culture?—but the Lord says the blessing may take *generations* to be fulfilled. We shouldn't stand around waiting for the blessing to come; we should get on with life and faithfully persevere. (Read Jer 29 in its entirety, and you may confirm that modern evangelicals have woefully misread this great passage.)

3. 1 Chronicles 4:9–10 has been misapplied

The "prayer of Jabez" (1 Chronicles 4:9–10) typifies the modern obsession with avoiding pain and striving for a comfy life. The fact that God granted Jabez's request (either preventing him from suffering or from inflicting pain, depending on the translation) doesn't entitle us to claim a cross-free, pain-free Christianity. God may have had his reasons for answering that particular prayer as he did. The passage may teach us about God's faithfulness, involvement in our lives, and so on, but it isn't intended as a model prayer. It is misleading to suggest that spiritual people can avoid pain, for often the spiritual are given a heavy load to bear. More often than not, we're required to drain the cup of suffering to its dregs (Matt 26:39).

Tell your friends what God's word says about the problem of evil! The biblical view connects with our hearts. So many skeptics have been turned off by syrupy expressions of faith. When believers trivialize suffering through sharing misapplied scriptures or offering platitudes, unbelievers feel justified for not believing. But they won't find it so easy to walk away when they hear the realistic diagnoses and gracious solutions found in Scripture.

Points to Remember:

- God isn't the creator of evil. Evil has no actual independent existence; it is merely the absence of good.
- Perhaps influenced by the world and the flesh, Christians have interpreted such passages as 1 Chr 4:9–10, Jer 29:11–14, and Rom 8:28 in such a way as to minimize the cross, and the necessity of faithful perseverance.

CHAPTER 24

The Cruciform Life
Letting Suffering Shape You

*A*s we saw in Rom 8:28–29, the Lord's plan includes pain. Yet this is hardly gratuitous suffering. Rather, pain borne for Christ's sake empowers us to be conformed to the character of Christ. Of course the change isn't automatic. Just surviving pain and complaining about it won't improve your heart; it may even degrade it. The operative word is *perseverance* (Rom 5:3–4).

God is all about relationships: his with us, ours with him, ours with family, fellow disciples, and outsiders. All relationships entail suffering. Think about it: marriage doesn't work without forgiveness, compromise, and sacrifice. Neither does parenting. Any close friendship is characterized by emotional pain: we will hurt each other. Don't believe people who claim never to have friction or disagreements; avoidance of real differences is hardly a healthy way to grow in friendship. This process of transformation isn't solely achieved in personal relationships, but for most of us this is the central arena where character is proved—and improved.

Another passage to consider is Phil 3:10–11. Being conformed to the image of Christ (Rom 12:2; 2 Cor 3:18) means we will learn to love as Christ loves. He will teach us. There's no way to this goal apart from suffering. Just as Jesus bore the cross (1 Pet 2:21–24), we too are called to carry a cross. And so cruciform (cross-shaped) living is the path of discipleship. The cruciform life is also a kind of crucible: impurities are burned off, and the precious gold or silver residue remains. The cruciform life enables us to love with less Self in the picture, fouling up the relationship.

How can I know whether I'm embracing the cruciform life?

Perhaps reading these thoughts on suffering has revealed some weaknesses in your own faith and theology. Do you need to reconsider the way you view suffering? Is it time to embrace the sufferings in your life as a vehicle for spiritual growth and transformation?

Jesus asked lots of questions to draw out people's hearts. Sometimes asking ourselves questions—taking a personal spiritual inventory—can shed light on where we are (2 Cor 13:5). Here are a few questions to ask yourself:

- *Have I been misreading biblical passages on suffering?* The Lord's agenda is our holiness, not our happiness.
- *Do I engage in relationships,* despite the risk of pain and disappointment? Isolation keeps us from conforming to the character of Christ.
- *Do I give of my wealth* even though I might prefer to use it to make my life more comfortable? Most believers live at the same standard of wealth as their neighbors.
- *Do I continue serving in my local church or house church,* even though I may not be not entirely happy with how things are run? Staying connected despite differences of viewpoint is a true mark of unity.
- *Do I say no gluttony and drunkenness?* Or do I eat/drink without caution or wisdom? It's not that food and wine are sinful, but over-indulgence is sin.

- *How is my track record in relationships?* Am I continually losing friends because of my selfishness (even though I want to blame others)? Have I allowed love to die—whether in a friendship, marriage, fatherhood, or motherhood? An objective third party wouldn't gloss over our serious character flaws, but we do it all the time. An honest appraisal of our relational history will reveal how seriously we are following God's plan for our lives.

- *Do I consider my life worth nothing* compared to knowing Christ, becoming like him in his death (Phil 3:7–10)?

Questions for the skeptic

Now that you've examined yourself, you're in a better position to ask questions of others, and to help them reconsider their views.

A skeptic criticizes God for not removing suffering from the world, but he (or she) doesn't have enough information to be confident in his allegation. He has no way of knowing what God might or might not do—and even less since he isn't experiencing the power of the cross at work in his life. After you present some of the arguments and clarifications in this chapter, ask your skeptic friend some questions like these:

- *Do you think Christianity offers simplistic solutions?* The Bible offers no cheap solution to make evil and suffering "all better." But it does speak of a place where God meets us in our suffering, demonstrating that he understands fully. That place is the cross. (You might also study the cross with your friend, or perhaps read a medical account of the crucifixion.)

- *Have you met "cotton candy" Christians*, whose conviction seems to be that we should smile our way through life without serious thought or authentic interaction? Are you any different from them, or are you also remaining at a shallow level in your thinking and relationships?

- *What are* you *doing to alleviate suffering in others' lives?* We are either part of the solution, or we're part of the problem.

I hope these chapters on suffering have helped you to think through theodicy with a nuanced and biblical perspective. I urge you to first take a look at your own attitude toward hardship and pain, and learn to embrace opportunities for growth, even when they are difficult. Resist the temptation to seek shallow theology and use misapplied scriptures as Band-Aids to make you feel better; instead, imitate Jesus: trust in the Father's care, and learn to grow through hard times. When you have that perspective, you will be better equipped to discuss the challenging topic of suffering with your skeptical friends.

Points to Remember:

- While there are many helpful biblical perspectives on the problem of suffering and evil—and these smooth the way so that we can have faith— true insight comes with personal experience of suffering.
- There's pain in the plan. If I am to learn to love others, my own selfishness needs to be burned away.
- Christ shows us the way. As he carried the cross daily (not only to Calvary), we too are called to cruciform living.

Part 1:
JESUS AND MIRACLES

It's no secret that Jesus was a controversial figure. In Part 7, Jesus and Miracles, we'll look at the difficulties skeptics have with Jesus. Did he actually exist? Was he divine, or just a remarkable rabbi? Did he have a nasty temper? What about the years he spent hanging out with the Buddha? Did the idea of his divinity develop later, after his death? And did he stay dead when he died . . . or not? We'll also respond to skeptics' questions about a related issue: miracles in the Bible.

CHAPTER 25

Who Was Jesus Really?

This chapter provides answers to twelve claims skeptics have made about Christ. If you learn these responses, you will be well equipped to defend the truth about Jesus Christ in nearly any situation.

1. "There's no proof Jesus even lived, apart from the Bible, which as we know is biased."

A recent Barna poll disclosed that in Britain only 61% believe Jesus was a real person.[27] This is demonstrably false, as a number of ancient non-Christians refer to Jesus.[28] Is it fair to rule out the Bible's words about Jesus, merely because they are favorable? Such thinking would lead us to reject any book written in praise (or censure) of anybody.

2. "Jesus' original words were lost by his disciples. No one can remember perfectly after a period of decades."

Ancient peoples, like a handful of modern ones, transmitted learning, wisdom, and culture through oral tradition. Jewish disciples were known to be adept at preserving a rabbi's teaching, especially through memorization. Though of course no one's memory is always perfect,

117

information is preserved well enough. For example, the blind poet Homer's *The Iliad* and *The Odyssey*—hardly short works!—have come down to us in this way. While there was a short oral phase in the transmission of the Jesus tradition, things were written down soon enough. And as long as his first followers were still alive, they were able to serve as a check on any significant errors in telling the gospel story.

3. "The New Testament was written too long after Jesus' life to be of historical value."

There was a period of about twenty years between the ascension of Christ (AD 30) and the first NT documents (Galatians, or possibly 1 Thessalonians). That's a pretty short time. For comparison, the definitive biography of Churchill did not come out in 1966 (the year after he died); some excellent volumes appeared in the 1980s and 1990s. In fact the passage of a few years was necessary to allow for perspective. But with the New Testament, we can get even closer than twenty years. Some sources about Christ cited in the NT go back to as close to Pentecost as two years, give or take (1 Cor 15:3–6)!

4. "Jesus' limited knowledge, as seen in Matthew 24:36, shows that he was not truly the Son of God."

Jesus was limited in various ways during his incarnation, so this should not surprise us. For example, he could be in only one place at a time, he grew tired, he had to eat in order to keep on going (apart from times of fasting), and he had presumably a normal human brain—no external hard drive for instant access to all the data in the universe. At times he used his divine powers, most often when he was helping others, but for the most part he seems to have lived without any unfair advantage that would remove him from the category of human being. The incarnation entailed an emptying of himself (Phil 2:7), including, apparently, a portion of his knowledge.

5. "Jesus taught the same things as Muhammad, Confucius, and all the other founders of world religions."

Not so. Careful scholarship has shown us that the differences between religions far outweigh the similarities. Have you ever read the Qur'an, the Hadith, or *The Analects of Confucius*? No one who has studied these works side by side with the Gospels can pretend that Jesus' message was the same as the others'. Rather, Jesus claimed to present and to be the exclusive truth (John 14:6). Others pointed to what they thought was the way; Jesus confidently proclaimed that he *is* the way.

6. "In the 'missing years,' Jesus traveled to India, sat at the feet of the Buddha and found enlightenment."

Not so. As a dutiful Jewish eldest son, in the "missing years" (ages twelve to thirty-two, years for which we have no information about his life), Jesus would have learned his father's craft. Once Joseph died, Jesus, as the eldest of five brothers (Matt 13:55), would have had family responsibilities— no time for a trip to India. Besides, the Buddha died nearly five centuries before Jesus was born! The teaching of Christ was not a form of Eastern mysticism, nor is it compatible with the views of other Asian religions, or the popular New Age Movement. Attempts to flatten the revolutionary teaching of Jesus, or homogenize the teachings of the world's religions, are misguided. To hear the voice of Christ, we must listen to him, not to those who would reinterpret him (2 Tim 4:3).

7. "Why should I follow someone given to temper tantrums (John 2:13–17), hate speech (Matthew 23:13–33), and anti-Semitism (John 8:39–47)?"

The "tantrum" was carefully calculated, conducted in a spirit of righteous indignation, and executed to signal the establishment that he was ready for the inevitable clash. Jesus said many hard things, but they were always tempered with love (Matt 23:37; Mark 10:21). While he did challenge the leaders of the Jews most forcefully—rightly so on account of their greater responsibility level—to accuse him, or any of his apostles, of anti-Semitism is silly. They were *all* Jews, after all!

8. "Jesus' divinity evolved. The earlier parts of the New Testament know nothing of his being God."

Actually, Jesus is clearly divine, equated with the Lord of the Old Testament and Jewish faith, in the very earliest strata of the NT. Later works expand on this insight, but Jesus is clearly divine in the earliest gospel, the beginning of Acts, the earliest letter, and the Apocalypse (Mark 1:1, 11, 24, 2:7; Acts 2:36; Rev 1:8). Every section of the NT points to him as deity.

9. "Thousands of manuscript errors have obscured the truth about Jesus. One person's guess is good as another's."

The copying errors are minor. No doctrine of Christianity is affected by a misspelling or a missing word here or there, especially when plenty of other ancient copies supplement what may be lacking. Copies of all ancient documents suffered some degree of degradation, but scholars don't for that reason automatically reject their contents. (For more on the manuscripts, review Part 2, The Scriptures.)

10. "The miracles of Christ were concocted by the church."

Jesus was a good person, and his teachings were good, and would be good even without the miracles. Then why did he stir up the wrath of the establishment? Why was he so loved and so hated? Christ was much more like the radical prophet Jeremiah than a mild-mannered rabbi. Removing the miracles from Christianity—miracles like the incarnation, the healings, and the resurrection—would leave nothing of substance, for it would mean that God did not visit our planet, he is unable to meet our needs, and we have no hope for life after death. Some miracles, especially the resurrection, vindicate Jesus' claims (Acts 17:31; Rom 1:4). Other signs tell us who Jesus is, like the miraculous signs running through the Gospel of John (2:11, 4:54, 5:9, 6:11, 6:19, 9:7, 11:44, 20:1–29). Discredit the central miracles in the life of Christ, and we might as well not be Christians (1 Cor 15:14–15, 19).

11. "Jesus only wanted us to be good people, not saints. He didn't require purity. He made out with his girlfriend, Mary Magdalene."

He certainly *did* insist that we lead holy lives (Matt 5:27–30). While Mary was one of his followers, the notion that he and Mary were involved is an idea much later than the first century. (You got this idea from Dan Brown's *The DaVinci Code*, right?) As for the idea of being good people, Jesus taught that no one can be good enough to be saved

(Mark 10:18). And all his followers *are* called to live holy lives—to be saints (Mark 8:34).

12. "I might believe if you could show me an example of someone who accepted Jesus' claims and miracles—as long as he wasn't a biased Christian."

The request doesn't really make sense, since anyone who accepted these things would certainly become a Christian! We can give you a long list of unbelievers and skeptics—in ancient times as well as in our own day—who were persuaded by the evidence. Besides, no one is completely unbiased, including the one making such a request.

Points to Remember:

1. **"There's no proof Jesus even lived, apart from the Bible."** False, disproved by a number of ancient Roman, Greek, Syrian, Jewish, and Christian sources.

2. **"Jesus' original words were lost."** Actually, the process of oral tradition in ancient cultures was more than adequate to preserve the record of Jesus' words and deeds. Further, the Jews were renowned for their careful preservation of tradition, oral and written alike.

3. **"The NT was written so long after Jesus' time that it has no historical value."** The NT began to be written some twenty years after Pentecost, and a few sources cited in the NT go back to about two years before Pentecost!

4. **"Jesus' limited knowledge proves he wasn't the Son of God."** Jesus' incarnation meant emptying himself, including part of his knowledge.

5. **"Jesus taught the same things as other religious founders."** Not so. Careful scholarship has shown us that the differences between religions far outweigh the similarities.

6. **"In the 'missing years,' Jesus traveled to India, finding enlightenment at the feet of the Buddha."** This is both implausible and impossible. *Implausible* because Jesus, the eldest of five brothers, would have had family

responsibilities—no time for a trip to India; *impossible* since the Buddha died five hundred years earlier.

7. **"Jesus often didn't act like a Christian."** Jesus said and did many hard things, but they were always tempered with love.

8. **"Jesus' divinity evolved."** Actually, every section of the NT points to him as deity, from the earliest strata (from the early 30s) to the latest (in the 90s).

9. **"Manuscript errors make the truth about Christ unknowable."** No doctrine of Christianity is affected by minor errors like misspellings or the odd missing word, especially with such a broad manuscript base. Historians seldom have access to such large numbers of ancient documents as Bible translators do!

10. **"The miracles of Christ were concocted by the church."** Removing the miracles from Christianity leaves nothing of substance in the biblical message, and certainly not a truthful message for which believers of all ages have been willing to die!

11. **"Jesus only wanted us to be good people."** All his followers *are* called to live holy lives—to be saints.

12. **"I might believe if I found an example of a contemporary non-Christian (not a believer) who accepted Jesus' claims and miracles."** That's illogical: anyone who believes in Christ is a believer, not a non-Christian!

CHAPTER 26
Did Jesus Stay Dead?

The resurrection is the linchpin of Christianity: If it's not true, then Jesus was not the Son of God, not who he said he was, and not a trustworthy teacher—the whole religion is a sham (1 Cor 15:15–19). In this chapter we will give rational responses to six objections skeptics often have to the resurrection.

1. "Jesus' resurrection was faked. His followers didn't want to give up on him, even when he failed, so to honor him they made up the story that he conquered death."

His followers (eyewitnesses) are unlikely to have been willing to die for something they knew was a lie. The Gospels depict their reluctance to stick their own necks out (John 20:18–19)—until they were convinced of his resurrection. Then they were transformed men! Besides, would they be honoring the one who insisted on telling the truth by fabricating his comeback from death? Hardly.

2. "Christ was a copy of other mythic figures, like Diogenes, Heracles, and Apollonius of Tyana."

The so-called parallels are too late and are poor "parallels." Scholars put the final nail into this coffin a century ago when the History of Religions School (a group of theologians connected to Germany's University of Göttingen in the late 1800s) roundly rejected this notion. Even so, this unsubstantiated allegation has been resurfacing of late.

3. "Other ancient divinities died and rose from the dead, so Christ's resurrection wasn't unique."

The pagan divinities typically died and rose annually, whereas Jesus' death and resurrection were one-time events (Heb 9:25–28). Unlike the pagan gods, Jesus rose with a resurrection body, and not in the underworld, but on the earth. Another important difference: his resurrection was not tied to annual agricultural cycles, but to our perennial need for a Savior.

4. "Jesus' followers, who were mainly women and slaves, found nothing strange in his coming back from the dead. After all, like other ancient people, they were superstitious and poorly educated."

Ancient people, including the lower classes (many of whom found a warm welcome in the church), knew as well as we do that people don't come back from the dead. The early church wasn't teaching that resurrection was a normal event! Their special claim was that Jesus was the first to conquer death, the first human resurrected in a new body (the "first fruits"), and that he is inviting us to follow him, with the assurance that we too will be resurrected, with the gift of immortality. Faith in this concept has nothing to do with the education level of church members.

5. "The Gospel accounts of the resurrection appearances are hopelessly confused. Why should I believe them?"

While each Gospel has its own emphases, all four agree that the tomb was empty. They agree that the resurrection was unexpected, even though Jesus had foretold it. And the disciples doubted. On all these points they are in perfect harmony. They are also in full agreement that the first witnesses to the resurrection were women. This is an especially telling point, since the testimony of women was not acceptable in a court of law. If the disciples were making the story up, it is doubtful they would have made the first witnesses female. But back to the incredulity of the disciples: why include this in an account written to persuade others of the resurrection? They are hardly presented as men of faith ready to take on the religious authorities! Once convinced, almost against their will, the disciples stand up for Christ, ready to die for him if necessary. These are some reasons you should believe them.

6. "The disciples experienced a group hallucination, perhaps triggered by their deep sadness over Jesus' death. Thus they were convinced that they had seen the risen Christ."
The appearances (see 1 Cor 15:5–7) were to individuals as well as to groups of various sizes. Normally when someone "sees" a dead person, the person making the appearance is dead. Yet in Jesus' case, they saw a *living* person. Nor was this just a fleeting glimpse of their dear departed friend. He had conversations with them, ate with them, and continued to instruct them—over a period of forty days (Acts 1:3)!

I'd like to close our section on Jesus Christ by recommending two of the best books on the resurrection I've ever read.

- The first is *The Case for the Resurrection of Jesus,* by Gary Habermas and Michael Licona (Kregel Publications, 2004). This book utilizes a "minimal facts" approach, emphasizing what can be known and agreed upon by the majority of scholars, believers or not. It's easy to read, and the accompanying CD includes a test, to see whether or not we've mastered the material. I highly recommend this work. These guys are a great team, and they definitely know their stuff.
- The second work is written at a scholarly level, superbly researched, though not for the faint of heart. The author is my friend Michael Licona, and the full title is *The Resurrection of Jesus: A New Historiographical Approach* (InterVarsity Press, 2010).

Let's all continue to grow in our ability to proclaim and defend the gospel (Phil 1:7)!

Points to Remember:

1. **"Jesus' resurrection was faked"**: A careful reading of the Gospels shows that the disciples lacked means, motive, and opportunity. This is most unlikely.

2. **"Christ was copied from mythological figures"**: The so-called "parallels" are too late, many appearing in manuscripts later than the NT. And the History of Religions School roundly rejected this notion a century ago!

3. **"The Resurrection is no different than other pagan 'resurrections'"**: Actually, it is very different. Christ rises once, not annually; the agricultural cycle is in no way linked to Christ's resurrection; he came back in a physical body to *this* world, not to the underworld; he was seen by many witnesses.

4. **"His followers were gullible"**: Jesus' followers knew as well as we do that people don't come back from the dead. It doesn't take a high level of education to tell the difference between resurrection and unsubstantiated rumor.

5. **"The Gospel accounts vary in the details, so the resurrection must be rejected"**: While the Gospels do exhibit different emphases, all agree on the basic points: death, burial, empty tomb, witnesses to the risen Christ.

6. **"Group hallucination"**: Sometimes the ghost of a loved one appears post-mortem, especially during a familiar routine. But Jesus' followers did not expect to see him. Further, they encountered him not a ghost, but as a living human. Would the "hallucination" appear to five hundred persons, or over a period of forty days?

CHAPTER 27

Is God a Lawbreaker?

*M*iracles are a key feature of the biblical story. For Christians, it is unthinkable that they are all spurious. The resurrection of Christ from the dead is the best news humankind has ever heard. (To be fair, the incarnation is a greater and even more central miracle.) Yet skeptics seldom allow the miracles. How shall we respond to the most common rejections of the miraculous?

Let's consider some of the prevailing objections to miracles:

1. "Miracles are impossible by definition."
Whose definition? One that precludes the supernatural? Science doesn't rule out the supernatural; it just can't access it, limited as science is to empirical reality. To me, as to the vast majority of mankind, reality appears to have two levels, an "upstairs" and a "downstairs." While we may not have direct (scientific) access to the upstairs, occasionally we hear sounds in the night, rumblings above. Is it really rational to dismiss the upper story out of hand, or the implication that it may be inhabited?

2. "All miracles are fake. They didn't happen in Bible times, and they don't happen today, either."

Given the abundance of fraudulent claims, we may find ourselves in agreement with the skeptic. I often suggest that ninety-nine percent of miraculous claims (outside the biblical record) are bogus, or else not supernatural. Psychosomatic healing is extremely common. At any rate, few miracles rank among the biblical wonders (restoring limbs, raising the dead, turning water to wine). For example, most people today who claim to have been healed are only "cured" of backaches, headaches, and so on. The adrenaline of the moment (in the arms of the healer) easily accounts for the (temporary) reprieve from pain. And yet for the one percent that are genuine, there is abundant and convincing testimony that God still answers prayer (Jas 5:16). Christians need to watch out lest their healthy skepticism undermine their faith in an all-powerful God.

3. "People living in pre-scientific Bible times were gullible. So of course they believed in miracles."

If that were true, how do we account for the refusal of so many to believe—and not just outsiders, but those within the family of faith as well? Actually, the average person living in "Bible times" never saw a sign or wonder. Dividing the number of recorded wonders into the number of years of biblical history, and then diluting the probability of witnessing a sign even further by taking account of the broad geographic spread of miracles (from Egypt to Israel to Asia Minor to Babylon and beyond), we realize that only a small percentage of believers who lived during Bible times ever saw a miracle. Most of them, like us, relied on the testimony of others. As for being unscientific, their worldview was certainly different from ours. And yet can we really believe that they expected people to walk on water, walk through fire unscathed, or rise from the dead? Of course not. There's no reason to believe they were less intelligent than us. We should beware cultural arrogance.

4. "The laws of nature are inviolable."

Why would miracles necessarily violate natural law? Maybe God's science is more advanced than ours! Maybe he harnesses laws or properties (as yet) unknown to us, or accelerates natural healing processes. After all, God is the one whose wisdom and order are reflected in natural law. Further, these laws are more *descriptions* of reality than *restrictions* of divine agency. The laws are not ironclad rules to which atoms, charges, and divine beings must submit.

There are no good reasons for rejecting miracles out of hand, and given the eyewitness testimony so central to the Christian message (2 Pet 1:16; 1 Cor 15:1–8; 1 John 1:1–3), there are strong reasons for paying attention to the miracles claimed in Scripture.[29]

Points to Remember:

- Of course, the skeptic is correct that miracles are impossible by definition—if you *define* them that way.
- Reality is composed of two "stories." The downstairs is the empirical world, subject to the examination of science. The upstairs is the invisible, non-physical, spiritual world. There is ample evidence for the reality of *both* stories.
- Miracles don't *violate* natural law. It may well be that God accelerates natural processes, or works *around* his laws.
- Pre-modern people weren't stupid; they did not passively accept all miraculous claims. For instance, they knew as well as we do that people don't walk on water—but *God* might (see Matt 14:25; Job 9:8).
- Few modern claims of the miraculous measure up to scrutiny, or to the quality level, of biblical miracle. Yet *some* do (perhaps one percent). When someone claims to have experienced or witnessed a miracle, we should be skeptical, though not excessively so.

Part 8:
WORLD RELIGIONS

We've spent most of the book considering ways to answer questions from people who are hesitant about faith, or have no faith whatsoever. In this section, World Religions, let's consider ways we can connect with people who *do* have faith—but faith in different religions.

The purpose of examining world religions is that we be both respectful and informed as we interact with members of other faith traditions (1 Pet 3:15). They are often skeptical of Christianity for different reasons than agnostics or atheists, and so they have different questions. The point of arming ourselves with knowledge isn't to insulate ourselves against other religions or to discredit them—but to prepare us for meaningful conversation. As believers in Christ, our mission is not to push outsiders away, but to reach out and share the truth of Christ with a confused world. We'll begin with Islam, and also take a look at various Eastern religions, the New Age trend, and Judaism.

CHAPTER 28

Basics of Islam: 5-4-3-2-1

*W*ith stories of terrorism and Islamic extremism so often in the news, many Christians have become fearful and mistrustful of their Muslim neighbors. Jesus crossed cultural barriers and reached out to people most of his fellow Jews distrusted and despised (see John 4; John 12:20–26; Luke 7:1–10). I encourage you to take the time to study and understand Islam and its followers, so that you might forge connections, and open up opportunities to share your faith.

Basic facts about Islam
- Islam's founder is Muhammad, who recited the *Qur'an* (also spelled *Koran*).
- The new religion began in Arabia, in the seventh century AD.
- Muslims believe the one true god is Allah.
- The Qur'an affirms Jesus' virgin birth, second coming, and miracles—even that he is the Word of God.
- Only a minority of Muslims speak Arabic. Most speak Indonesian, Bengali, Urdu, Turkish, Farsi, and a few other tongues.

- Most do not live in the Middle East. In fact, more than half live in Indonesia, India, Pakistan, and Bangladesh.
- Nearly twenty-five percent of the planet is Muslim—that's one in four persons!

Islam by the numbers

And that brings us to our topic: Islam by the numbers. There are a few numbers to master, if you want to be in the know concerning the basics of Islam. We'll keep it simple, and take the approach of a countdown: 5–4–3–2–1.

Five pillars

What does it take to become and live as a Muslim? Our first number is *five*—as in the Five Pillars of Islam. The countdown will continue as we touch on the place of women, the Trinity, major factions, and Allah.

1. *Confession:* That Allah is the one God and Muhammad is his messenger. This is how one becomes a Muslim—sort of like the "Sinner's prayer" of many Protestant Christians.
2. *Prayer:* Five times daily, facing Mecca. Originally the direction was towards Jerusalem, but when the Jews rejected Muhammad's message, he changed the city.
3. *Alms:* giving to the needy is also required, about two percent of one's income (Sunni Muslims) or twenty percent (Shiites).
4. *Fasting:* A daylight fast during the Muslim month of Ramadan. Since Muslims follow a lunar calendar (354 days in the year), Ramadan rotates through the Western solar calendar.
5. *Pilgrimage:* Once in one's lifetime one should try to visit the holy city of Mecca.
6. Some would add a sixth pillar, jihad (which we will discuss in the next chapter).

Remember: Five pillars, CPAFP.

"Confession–Prayer–Alms–Fasting–Pilgrimage" may be easier to recall with an acronym. How about Camels Pursuing A Familiar Path, or Certified Public Accountant Financial Peace? I frequently rely on mnemonics. (Easier to rely on them than on a faulty memory—do you relate?)

Four wives

Despite the considerable overlap between Islam and Judaism and Christianity, there are many points at which the Qur'an is in severe tension with the gospel. It's not just the rejection of the crucifixion and resurrection of Christ, but also the view of grace, the treatment of enemies, and the rights of women.

The Qur'an permits men to take up to four wives (sura 4:3). What we as outsiders may not realize is that most Muslims are monogamous. Having multiple wives is expensive! Thus polygamy serves as a status marker. Interestingly, Muhammad had far more than just four. When Muhammad wanted a woman, Allah permitted him directly to take her, even if she was already married.

Another troubling verse is 4:34: "Men are the protectors and maintainers of women, because Allah has given the one more (strength) than the other, and because they support them from their means. Therefore the righteous women are obedient . . . As to those women on whose part you fear disloyalty and ill-conduct, admonish them (first), (Next) refuse to share their beds, (And last) beat them (lightly). . . ."

I suppose we all need a word of admonition now and again. Yet what about withholding conjugal rights, or employing violence (even if it is only a light slap on the face)?

Remember: Four wives, sura 4.

Three gods (False Trinity)

The version of Christianity Muhammad was exposed to was quite different from the original, apostolic faith. Two centuries earlier the church had ruled that Mary is the mother of God (Council of Ephesus, AD 431). Many prayed to her. And thus it appeared that Christians worshipped three gods. The "Trinity" was Allah, Mary, and Jesus (4:171 and 5:73).

Certainly Christians, like Muslims, affirm the unity of God. We are not tri-theists (those who worship three gods). Muhammad was certainly reacting to the lapsed, worldly version of Christianity current in Arabia in the seventh century.

Remember: "Three gods" (false trinity)

Two major divisions

Muslims do not constitute a monolithic faith. Through the centuries they have divided and subdivided. Some follow some certain traditions, others different ones. Not surprisingly, there is even more than one version of the Qur'an. Some Muslims are mystics; the Sufis long to experience the God of love (pretty much absent from mainstream Islam). They seek ecstatic union with Allah, and even speak in "tongues." Last, American readers, please note that the Nation of Islam is not considered legitimate by Muslims, since it is a racial movement (for African-Americans), and holds to a number of un-Islamic ideas.

The *two* main divisions are Sunni and Shi'a Islam. Shi'ites differ from their mainstream cousins on many doctrines and practices, and the break goes back to the death of Muhammad (AD 632). Shi'ites hold that the succession of the caliphate ought to come through the family of the prophet—through Muhammad's son-in-law Ali. Not so the Sunnis! Shi'ites are perhaps fifteen percent of all Muslims, while eighty percent are Sunnis. Shi'ites are most common in Iran and Iraq, but also proliferate in Pakistan and India; Sunnis, everywhere else.

Remember: Many flavors, but two major groupings, Sunnis and Shi'ites.

One god

Of course there is only *one* deity in Islam, and that is Allah (the Arabic name for god). Interestingly, in Islam the unforgivable sin is "associating" any other being with God. Suggesting that Allah has a wife, or a child, or that a human could be God (like Jesus) is blasphemy. So the incarnation (God became flesh) is no minor difference between the Muslims and the Christians. The Christian affirms that the Word became flesh (John

1:14); the Muslim denies it and cries "heresy!" Thus it is no exaggeration to state that the central teaching of Christianity is the unforgivable sin of Islam.

Remember: One God, Allah.

5–4–3–2–1
Putting it all together, we have:

- 5 pillars—CPAFP
- 4 wives—sura 4
- 3 gods—false trinity
- 2 divisions—Sunni and Shi'a
- 1 God—Allah

If you'd like a "bonus" number, Muslims have *six* articles of faith: God; the prophets (including Jesus); the Scriptures (the Law, Psalms, Gospel, and Qur'an, given by Moses, David, Jesus, and Muhammad); angels; the judgment day; and destiny.[30]

CHAPTER 29

Jihad

*I*n 2014 Boko Haram, the West African ultra-radical group opposed to all things Western (except guns), kidnapped hundreds of Nigerian schoolgirls. On one of their notorious raids, they carried off sisters from my own fellowship, the Churches of Christ. The goal: forced conversion, followed by sale as brides.

Would that this were a rare occurrence. Thanks to groups like Boko Haram and their radical partners, ISIS, such atrocities are weekly news. But is this really representative of the faith? Didn't we hear somewhere that "Islam" means peace? Wouldn't the gentle prophet Muhammad roll over in his grave if he witnessed such deeds perpetrated in his name?

This chapter asks you to consider whether or not violence is a historical part of the Muslim faith. The goal is neither offense nor fearmongering, but clarity. When we're thinking clearly, we're less reactionary, better able to listen, and more likely to make a connection with the twenty-five percent of the planet who are Muslim.

Violence in Islam?

Most Muslims long for peace—we should not doubt that. I've met hundreds of Muslims, perhaps thousands (especially in the Middle East, Asia, and Africa), but never a violent one. Yet some consider *jihad* a fundamental duty of all Muslims, the "sixth pillar" of Islam. *Jihad* is Arabic for *striving*: sometimes this refers to striving for justice or righteousness, but usually it refers to a violent struggle to establish Islam as the global religion of mankind.

Granted, the *jihadis* and their supporters are a minuscule fraction of the whole. However, given nearly two billion adherents, even a fraction of one percent equates to millions of potential terrorists. That's a strong reason for us to be informed. Further, *Islam* does not mean *peace*. It means *submission*. The word itself is an ultimatum.

In this chapter we will see that there is a violent strand within Islam, and its roots are historical (Islamic practice), scriptural (the Qur'an), and personal (the life of Muhammad, recounted in the Hadith).

War and Peace

Converts were few in the early years (starting in AD 610), but once Muhammad authorized attacks on caravans, compelling people to join the movement or suffer the consequences, the numbers began to swell. Not that Islam always spread by the sword. To be fair, it has also spread through commerce and a prolific birthrate. Yet the Muslim Conquest received its impetus from the sword. The 600s–800s, from Afghanistan to Spain, were centuries of explosive growth.

The vision of a Muslim world was not only fueled by desire for booty, but also facilitated by simplistic thinking. The entire world fell into two categories: the house of Islam and the house of war. You're with us or you're (potentially) against us. The house of Islam are the faithful. The infidels—the house of war—will face hellfire. Some Muslim scholars add a third house, the house of peace, *Dar es Salaam* (like the large city in Tanzania, across from Zanzibar).

But isn't this just history? Some Muslims may have taken up the sword, but does that prove violence is intrinsic to the faith? After all, many Christians have attacked their enemies; does this mean that Jesus sanctioned their actions? Good point.

It is written . . .

Let's go to the sources. Compare the teachings of Jesus with those of Muhammad. Read the following passages, selected from the Qur'an (Q), the Hadith, and the Gospels, and decide whether you think the founders of Christianity and Islam shared the same view on force and violence.

- Jesus said, "Father, forgive them, for they know not what they are doing." (Luke 23:34)
- And slay them wherever you find them, and drive them out of the places whence they drove you out. (Q 2:190)
- "If anyone strikes you on the right cheek, turn to them the other cheek also." (Matthew 5:39)
- I will instill terror into the hearts of the unbelievers. (Q 8:12)
- For he who insults you [Muhammad] will be cut off. (Q 108:3)
- "Take my yoke upon you, and learn from me, for I am gentle and humble in heart." (Matthew 11:29)
- Allah's apostle said, "I have been ordered to fight the people till they say, 'None has the right to be worshiped but Allah.' " (the Hadith of Bukhari 8.387)
- Killing disbelievers is a small matter to us. (the Hadith of Tabari IX.69)
- "Love your enemies and pray for those who persecute you." (Matthew 5:44)

I've read the entire Qur'an several times. In addition, I've spent dozens of hours scouring the Hadith. Here I learned that Islam permits killing, maiming, starving, and abusing one's enemies; dispatching one's enemy in order to confiscate his property (your actions are vindicated if you can *prove* he was your enemy); execution of (male) apostates; killing those who, presented with the choice, refuse to convert; executing adulterers; amputating limbs, per *Shari'a* law, *sometimes* with anesthetic; torture; slavery; wife beating; revenge; and cursing. Although Muslims cite the verse, "There shall be no compulsion in religion" (Q 2:256), this is not how the faith has played out historically, nor is it an entirely accurate depiction of Islam in the twenty-first century.

No cartoons, please

The truth is, Muhammad was a warrior. He killed his enemies and even executed those who mocked him. The Qur'an frequently threatens hellfire: in four percent of cases, for serious sin; but in ninety-six percent of the verses, for merely disagreeing with Muhammad. Freedom of speech has been a weakness within Islam from the very beginning. To insult Muhammad is to insult Allah; it is blasphemy. Yet when Jesus was insulted, or treated unjustly, he did not lash back (Matt 26:52–54; 1 Pet 2:21–23).

Consistency

Maybe it's best not to compare Muslims with Christians—let alone the worst of Islam with the best of Christianity (a common yet unfair tactic). Let us rather compare Muhammad and Jesus. How did they live? How did they treat their enemies?

The four gospels tell us all about Jesus. For Muslims, little is learned of Muhammad in the Qur'an (which actually names Jesus more than it mentions Muhammad). They rely therefore on the Hadith. These are the thousands of recollections of the words and actions of Muhammad. They are interesting, since they give us a real-life picture of the prophet of Islam. If you think the Qur'an is violent, just read the Hadith!

Some counter that Jesus violently attacked the temple (John 2), yet there is no evidence that he harmed anybody. Others point out the "sword" of Matthew 10:34. Yet this sword is clearly figurative, bringing relational division, not bloodshed. The Prince of Peace turns swords into plowshares; the Messianic age is one of peace. Even in the Apocalypse, Christ's sword isn't a literal sword, but the powerful word of God (Rev 1:16; 2:12, 16; 19:15; see Heb 4:12).

So when Christians are violent, they act in spite of what Jesus taught. Violence is inconsistent with Christ. But when Muslims resort to force, they are imitating Muhammad's personal example, obeying his directives. Several centuries after Pentecost, Christians used compulsion, resorted to violence, were increasingly intolerant, and would eventually authorize torture to maintain doctrinal uniformity. But they were *ignoring* Jesus' message, not following it. Herein lies the difference between faith in Christ and faith in Allah and his messenger Muhammad.

Some Christians would go further, denying that Allah is God at all. Certainly there are major differences. Allah does not love sinners. He is Monarch, not Father. Yet we must be careful not to exaggerate the differences. To be fair, Miroslav Volf, arguing that the Muslim and Christian gods may be identified, makes several insightful and balanced points in his book *Allah: A Christian Response* (HarperOne, 2011). At the very least, however, it holds true that the way we perceive God affects how we treat our fellow human beings.

The bottom line
Islam is not peace. It is submission. Indeed, as the Bible says in Isaiah and Philippians, "every knee will bow" to God (Isa 45:23; Phil 2:10). Yet the Bible makes it clear that this submission may not take place in this life, and certainly not at sword-point. It's not our job to force conversion. If we have the truth, we ought to have faith that the word will achieve its purpose (Isa 55:11). We need to leave outcomes to the Lord, not take things into our own hands (1 Cor 3:6).

Ignorant, uninformed, or careless?
No follower of Christ wants to be ignorant, uninformed, careless, or unloving. We want the cross to draw the world to Christ (John 12:32), not push them away.

CHAPTER 30
Connecting with Muslims

*G*rowing up in Florida and New Jersey, I was brought up around Christians and Jews. I never met a Muslim until I was twenty-three, as a student in Europe. When I led Bible discussions at the University of London, it was often the Muslims who turned out in droves. They were proud of their religion, critical of the West, and passionate. As it dawned on me that this was an important religion, my interest grew. At twenty-four, I spent a month in Muslim-majority Malaysia, visiting my first mosque.

Fast-forward twenty years, to terrorism in the news, the West alarmed by 9/11, and clerics issuing *fatwas* (in effect, death decrees) against those who "insult" Islam. Not surprisingly, when I first started producing materials on Islam, I was anxious. But in spite of my initial fears, the Islamic world hasn't batted an eye at my writing and teaching. Probably I'm not important enough to merit censure. Or perhaps it's because I've striven to show respect, and spent a lot of time reading the Qur'an, that they have welcomed me. As for the countries where I could get into real trouble—well, since my views on Muhammad are public, those places may not grant me a visa anyway.

I've been able to write a book on Islam, debate an imam, engage Muslim intellectuals on university programs, and speak in twenty nations with large Muslim populations. I teach about Islam at Lincoln Christian University, and network with brothers and sisters evangelizing in the Muslim quarter of the world, hoping somehow to be a resource for them. Now and again I bring a Muslim to church. Though of course I'm cautious, overall I'm relaxed in my witness to Muslims. My head is still on my shoulders. (Not to make light of those who have lost theirs.)

All this to say: Now that you're aware, don't be afraid to connect! Most of us are more likely to be ignored than persecuted. Many Muslims react positively when they learn the truth about Jesus Christ. We who understand the gospel have an obligation (1 Cor 9:19; Rom 1:14).

Evangelistic strategies

So what should our strategy be? Is it enough only to be informed? Of course not. All I can do is make a few suggestions; they will have to be general. Every person is different, every situation requires its own approach.

Avoid sensationalism; spend time with a Muslim

There's a lot of chatter about terrorism, and such talk will nearly always be more interesting than the mundane side of Islam. Most Muslims are peace-loving. Let it not be said of us that Islamophobia has become the new anti-Semitism. Hatred, bitterness, objectifying others—these are not Christian virtues. When we fail to see others as fellow humans, it's easy to misrepresent, blame, and ultimately to avoid them. We may end up with an Israel/Palestine divide: neither side talking with the other, let alone sharing their faith. A personal relationship with someone of another faith goes a long way in breaking down barriers.[31]

Search for common ground

Of course we ought not to be naive about the substantial differences between Islam and Christianity. *Shirk*, the association of any other being with Allah, is the unforgivable sin of Islam. On such an understanding, for a Muslim, Jesus cannot be the Son of God. Grace in Islam seems to be merited rather than freely received. And yet there is much common ground between the two faiths. Consider the unity of God, the day of judgment, or even the need for submission. (All Christians believe in obedience, or *Islam*, in this sense.) Emphasizing only our differences will lead to a standoff; stressing only our similarities is naive and only conceals significant differences that deserve discussion. Strive for balance.

Talk about Allah

Muslims and Christians agree that God is one. He is powerful, majestic, omniscient, and just. He deserves and demands our obedience. In the 600s, Muhammad challenged a largely polytheistic Arabia to renounce idolatry and embrace the true God. (Had Jews and Christians in the peninsula grown lukewarm in their outreach?) Yet Allah is more monarch than father, more commander than friend. Christians frequently underemphasize God's authority, so the Muslims have a point when they emphasize his strength—yet at the cost of a personal relationship with the Lord. Allah is simply too lofty, distant, aloof. He would never live in our hearts.

Among his "99 names" are Avenger, Afflicter, Lord of Retribution, Bringer of Death, Humiliator, and Subduer. Most of these have biblical counterparts. Allah is also Compeller, which doesn't harmonize well with the oft-quoted verse claiming there's no compulsion in religion (2:256). And yet Christians believe that at the last day it will be too late to choose; God will "compel" us. (Maybe it's more accurate to say that judgment is the result of our own choices.) The Qur'an says, "Allah is the best of deceivers" (3:54). That doesn't sound good, yet then again there's 2 Thess 2:11, where God sends a "powerful delusion" to those who refuse to accept the truth. But who ultimately chooses? The Islamic doctrine of fate dictates a strong determinism. Most Christians are (rightly) uncomfortable with a deity who predestines every decision.

I find that the Qur'an, rather than wholly lacking a biblical conception of God, is many times nearly biblical. Yet it stresses the more frightening aspects of God, while omitting most of his comforting and personal ones. The imams might disagree with me, and I admit my perception is subjective. I want to be fair, not to paint Allah in darker colors than is warranted. And yet frequently Allah doesn't feel like the God and Father of our Lord Jesus Christ (Rom 15:6).[32]

Talk about Jesus

Not only should we talk about God; we should also focus on Jesus. The Muslims honor Jesus in their own way: They view him as a prophet, second only to Muhammad; he is miracle-working, sinless, born of a virgin, the Messiah, the one to come again at the last day. He is mentioned more often in the Qur'an than Muhammad. He is the Spirit of God and even the Word of God (4:171). Ponder this last point: God, Word of God, Spirit of God—there's a Trinity in the Qur'an!

And yet Islam misses the central truth about Christ: he is God in the flesh. Further, the cross has caused offense and thus been dismissed (1 Cor 1:18–23). What prophet ends up executed? Weakness is a sign of value, unworthy of Muhammad, unthinkable of Allah. Surely Allah protects his messengers from harm. (So the Muslims reason.) Yet Christians know a God who stoops down to make us great. He took on human flesh (Phil 2). This sort of weakness is actually strength (2 Cor 12:9, 13:4)! And so we see that God is greater than Allah.

Mainstream Muslims reject Jesus' crucifixion and resurrection, which is the very heart of the gospel (1 Cor 15:1ff). Yet the Qur'an states that Christians should follow the gospel, or *Injil* (Q 5:46–47).

Be respectful; appreciate the stakes

Christ-followers are called not only to proclaim the faith, defending it with their intellect and, if need be, their lives (Rev 12:11). We are also to do so with respect (1 Pet 3:15; 2 Tim 2:23–26). Part of respect is appreciating the dishonor that attaches to becoming a Christian—especially to the act of baptism— for most Muslims. It's the ostracism of the blind man (John 9) on steroids. Most Muslims are part of close-knit families and communities. Conversion often means disinheritance. It certainly means loss of friends. In many places it means automatic incarceration, if not execution. The psychological block to conversion is enormous, dwarfing the minor challenges we in the West may face when we take a stand for Christ.

Historical perspective is also helpful, and explains the shame and humiliation that drive radical behavior. For a period of centuries, the caliphate enjoyed not only political power, but also some degree of cultural superiority. The Europeans, by comparison, were backward people. Once the caliphate became strong, it was even reported that Muhammad said, "The ink of the scholar is holier than the blood of the martyrs." Yet the caliphate slowly disintegrated. Soon after World War I it dissolved completely. As we know, some Islamists today seek to reestablish it: not so much to create the caliphate as to recreate it, to regain what was lost.

Islam was born six hundred years after Christianity. Six hundred years ago, what were the religious freedoms and democratic rights of the common man in Europe? Not all that great. True, we find extreme backwardness in the area of politics, human rights, and even infrastructure in the contemporary Muslim world. Yet when we go back six hundred years to consider the religious intolerance and patriarchy of Europe in the early 1400s—comparing apples to apples—Europe has nothing to be proud of! "Democratic" traditions aren't easy to build. The Muslims had a late start; perhaps we shouldn't be condescending.

Be faithful; reach out

Have you ever reached out to a Muslim? It's not that hard to do, especially if you live in Europe or the Americas. Have you ever baptized a Muslim? That's more difficult. (I have, though I want to do more.) Yet today multitudes of Muslims are coming to Christ. This even includes some imams! I met a newly baptized sister in the Middle East a few months ago—what a joy! I know brothers with a Muslim background who are laboring to make a difference in the world, like my friend George, founder of SALT Impact (Serving Arabs Leadership Team, an organization devoted to sharing Christ with Muslims). I have friends dedicated to the dangerous work of reaching Muslims in the territory contested by Al Qaeda and ISIS.

Jesus sought out those at the margins, those who were misunderstood, those from whom others kept their distance. Doesn't the promise of John 12:32 apply to Muslims? When they see Jesus lifted up, will not they too be drawn to him?[33]

Don't stop now

It's time to connect. Don't wait till you're some kind of an expert on Islam, or your company transfers you to Dubai. Act now. Continue to learn, but as you learn, reach out to Muslims in your community.

I hope this approach to engaging with the world's second-largest religion can serve as a model for how to approach other faiths: know the basic facts, be respectful, reach out, show the love of Christ.

CHAPTER 31

2500 Gods

One of the more unusual books in my library is Michael Jordan's *Encyclopedia of Gods: Over 2,500 Deities of the World.* (No, not *that* Michael Jordan!) Now the book doesn't cover all the gods worshiped in the course of human history. For example, nowhere could I locate my favorite, Chrysosandaliaimopotichthonia, the blood-sucking goddess of the underworld who wears golden sandals. Apparently the encyclopedia is abridged—just the top 2500 made it in!

There are way too many deities to cover; our brief survey of religions can't offer more than a sampling of world faiths. Through the last few chapters, you've gotten a broad-strokes understanding of Muhammad and his god, Allah. Next we'll look at Yahweh (the Lord revealed in the Judeo-Christian scriptures). In this chapter, we turn to the religions of the East.

The spectrum of belief

The plurality of human beings is nominally Christian. Sadly, only a minority of these are walking on the narrow road (Matt 7:13–14), as insiders and outsiders alike agree. To illustrate, the latest statistics show that only seventeen percent of the residents of the United States attend church in an average week, although the vast majority self-report as Christian.[34]

Christianity falls into several major groupings: Protestant, Catholic, Orthodox, Pentecostal. Each comprises hundreds of millions of members—yet so do several of the larger world faiths. Please see the chart at douglasjacoby.com, search phrase "Graphic 1."

Muslims constitute nearly one in four persons alive today; Hindus, one in five; and Buddhists, one in fourteen. Since these last two groups combined take in more than twenty-five percent of human beings, that's where we'll focus in this chapter.

Note that although secular or state atheism isn't an organized religion, it's still significant: one in ten persons live in this environment. Further, many religious persons are "practical atheists." That is, despite the trappings of religion, they live as though there were no God (Titus 1:16; Ps 14:1).

East meets West

Scholars of religion distinguish Eastern and Western religions. Yet "East" is a relative term: east of what? The phrase is Eurocentric (east of London, Paris, or Berlin). Originally, Near East meant Israel, Jordan, Lebanon . . . ; Far East referred to Japan, Korea, China . . . ; and while Middle East *should be* India, Pakistan, Afghanistan, today "Middle" East usually refers to Egypt, Israel, Saudi Arabia . . .

To add to the muddle, *every* major world religion was founded in Asia, so all are Eastern (Oriental), not Western (Occidental). Israel (the birthplace of Judaism and Christianity) and Arabia (the birthplace of Islam) are in Southwest *Asia*. Yet academics typically consider Europe Western. Now that that's been clarified (or not), what are the differences between Eastern and Western religions?

God

In the East, there are multiple deities. Gods and goddesses are typically more human than holy, engaging in selfish, violent, or sexual behavior. Like us, they too are trapped in the cycle of reincarnation

(Hinduism and popular Buddhism). Western religions acknowledge *one* god.

In the East, since there's no hard distinction between deity and nature, everything is "divine." Mother Earth is both alive and divine (as in the blockbuster movie *Avatar*). True, Christians acknowledge that we may partake in God's own nature, yet this is at his invitation, and requires holy living according to his word (2 Pet 1:3–10, 3:14–18). Yet we are not God.

Truth

In the East, one seeks truth *within*. In the West, truth lies without. Humans aren't inherently good, or even neutral; we are sinful. The East looks inward for subjective truth; the West reaches out for objective truth.[34]

Repentance

The East says that since we are divine, yet don't know it, our underlying problem is ignorance, not sin. Thus repentance has little place in the Eastern faiths. The way of deliverance lies in knowledge, not repentance. But biblical enlightenment is primarily moral, not intellectual (John 3:19–21).

Scripture

In Eastern religions, scriptures aren't so important. They aren't the touchstone by which everything else is to be evaluated. Not to say the East is without them; the Hindus have more than 100,000 pages of scripture, while the Buddhist sacred writings run to 200,000 pages—200 times the length of the Bible!

Reason

In Eastern religions, reason *interferes* with spiritual progress. So it is with meditation. Whereas in Christianity (and Judaism), we should *fill* our minds with the word of God (Josh 1:8; Ps 1:2; Phil 4:8; Col 3:16), in effect the Eastern monks *empty* theirs. In the West, reason is central to knowing God's thoughts. To many Eastern and New Age practitioners, like Eckhart Tolle (*A New Earth*), sophisticated talk doesn't need to be coherent. Contradiction is embraced, even when the result is nonsense!

Time
In the East, time is cyclical, not linear. This life is not particularly special, just one segment in a recurring series. Hence the doctrine of reincarnation, where one has, in effect, multiple chances at salvation.

Salvation
In Hinduism, the goal is to be reborn at a higher level, and one day to escape the unceasing cycles of reincarnation. Then one's liberated soul becomes one with the "world soul," like a drop of water returning to the sea. All will be one.

In classical Buddhism, in contrast, the goal is to realize that one has no soul— no individual existence at all. If Hinduism has all being one, Buddhism has all being nothing. In neither case will there be a personal relationship with God—or with anybody else, for that matter. You can't get much farther from biblical religion than these scenarios!

The cross
Since the gods don't care about us, and our fundamental problem isn't sin, Eastern religions have no place for the cross. Christianity alone grasps that the one God became flesh, bore our sins, and provided redemption. I have discussed this fact with several priests, monks, gurus, rabbis, and imams. None can offer anything approaching the cross of Christ! No incarnation, crucifixion, resurrection—and mankind is "without hope and without God" (Eph 2:12).

Western religions
- Judaism — Israel, monotheistic
- Zoroastrianism — Persia, dualistic: God and the devil are equally powerful.
- Christianity — Israel, monotheistic

- Islam — Arabia, monotheistic, drawing heavily on Judaism and Christianity

Eastern religions (especially Indian)
- Hinduism — India; common wherever Indians have migrated
- Buddhism — India; spread throughout Asia (died out in India)
- Jainism — India; originating (like Buddhism) in Hinduism
- Sikhism — India; a sort of blend of Hinduism and Islam
- Taoism — China
- Confucianism — China
- Shinto — Japan
- Baha'i — Persia (Iran)

You can learn more about these faiths by perusing the scriptures of the Eastern religions.

Superstitions from the East?

Isaiah 2:6 says, "They are full of superstitions from the East..." Sometimes people (including Christians) get confused when considering the merits of Eastern religions. Some Eastern traditions exhibit exemplary self-control. They encourage disciplined bodies, and who doesn't want that? Further, some of the most respectful persons I've ever met have been Buddhist monks. Some people have taken their admiration to a whole new level, wondering if the Dalai Lama might possess the Spirit of Christ. They begin to think that maybe we're over-analyzing, or just being "judgmental." Is one's choice of faith really a big deal?

Actually, it is. We've already considered a number of the logical, moral, and theological problems with the Eastern faith traditions (previous section). Still, many in the West are drawn to the East. Why is this?

The notion that we are gods is a mirage—a lie promoted by the enemy ever since Eden (Gen 3:1–5)—yet it's an attractive lie. It flatters the ego. But reality doesn't simply adapt to meet the whims of the enlightened individual, nor does it guide us along our way (as though the world had a soul or were intelligent). This naive view continues to promote itself in New Age fiction, such as *The Celestine Prophecy* (James Redfield) and *The Alchemist* (Paulo Coelho).

Many Westerners are disillusioned with church. Eastern superstitions offer an alternative. They may make us feel good, or provide elite knowledge. The "reality" they proclaim may feel more substantial than the anemic spirituality of so-called Christianity. However, the substance (reality) is found in Christ (Col 2:18)!

Eastern religions, including the New Age Movement, don't come with a warning label. Yet the mistaken belief that truth is flexible sets us up for failure. Seeking the truth "within" renders us susceptible to narcissism, as well as mind-altering drugs (think the groovy 1960s), alcoholism (a way of life for many in the West), or irresponsible escape from reality in virtual worlds (think high-tech games). Yet the true God calls us to live in the real world.

If the superstitions from the East were correct, or even coherent, then who would Jesus be?

- A bigot who saw black-and-white, although reality is completely gray.
- A person unable to give his life for our salvation.
- A guru at best, a fraud at worst—and certainly not divine in any unique way.

Let's not be taken in by "superstition from the east." God's people were susceptible during the days of Isaiah. We also should be on our guard, even against the influence of New Age novels and films. Let us rely upon God's unchanging word as we search for truth and direction for life.

As we shall see in the next chapter, biblical Judaism—the predecessor of the Christian faith—is radically different from the Eastern religions. It reveals the true God (there's only one—not 2500!). Judaism provides the bedrock foundation for the way of Jesus Christ.

CHAPTER 32

Judaism: A Revolutionary Religion

*I*n this chapter we move from India (Hinduism, Buddhism) westward, to the land of Israel (Judaism). As we'll see, the truths revealed to the Jews three millennia ago weren't just progressive; they were absolutely unique in the ancient world!

The revolutionary truths we study in this chapter will be useful in your outreach, especially in countering ill feeling about "the God of the Old Testament." More than that, once you've grasped these exciting principles, you'll be better able to free others up emotionally and intellectually, so that they may be drawn to God!

The revolutionary truths of Judaism
There are at least ten ways in which Judaism was surprisingly ahead of its time and far superior to all alternatives (the contemporary religions of Egypt, Babylon, Persia, Greece, the land of Canaan, etc.).

1. One God. Ancient religions were polytheistic. These gods had their own agendas, often less than noble. Yet Judaism is monotheistic; the god of the Old Testament (*Yahweh*, in the original Hebrew) brooks no rivals. It is true that in the Bible we find numerous allusions to the familiar pagan myths. Yet these myths (creation, the flood, etc.) are rejected—rewritten and scrubbed clean of paganism. Did you know that Judaism was the only monotheistic religion?

2. A Holy God. For most early religions, gods and goddesses were powers of nature personified. They resembled oriental kings—in effect, super-humans. Not so with Yahweh! He is holy, and his holiness isn't just a matter of degree. He is wholly above and beyond us humans. Yet he invites us to share in his holiness. Revolutionary, indeed!

3. No idolatry. No images of the Jewish God were permitted, even in the Holy of Holies. Whereas pagan temples always had a statue, Israel had only the ark of the covenant—a kind of throne for the invisible Yahweh. As for the image, *humans* display the image of God. Instead of a statue of the deity being paraded through the streets, *we* represent our Lord to the watching world.

4. Relational faith. God doesn't manipulate us, nor can we manipulate him. True religion is neither mechanical nor magical; it's relational. God wants to live with us, and within us. This also means that ethics are central; Yahweh is concerned with the heart. Religion without righteousness is worthless.

5. Sabbath. Humans are neither animals nor machines; hence the cycle of work is punctuated with a deliberate rest. In Egypt the Hebrew slaves didn't have a "weekend"—no day off. When they received the Torah, all this changed. Unbelievers ridiculed the Jews for not working nonstop. But for the Jews, Sabbath was a time for family, to reflect on God's word, to ensure Yahweh was central in the life of the community. Regardless of how we understand the fourth commandment, Sabbath is still vital for us today. God's people rejected the world's crazed emphasis on production. Do we?

6. Separation of priesthood and politics. To protect against the corruption that inevitably occurs when politics and religion mix, God established a safeguard based on tribe. Priests (descended from Levi) couldn't be kings, and kings (from the tribe of Judah) couldn't be priests. In contrast, among the pagans, the king might officiate as a priest, and some even claimed divinity. The state prophets enforced his sometimes capricious decrees. In Judaism, this was reversed: prophets challenged kings!

7. Separation of worship and sex. Pagan religions glorified ritual prostitution (both male and female) in their temples. In Hebrew religion, sex was pure, set exclusively in the context of marriage. Marriage was honored; homosexuality, bestiality, and incest were forbidden. Not so among the pagans. For example, the highly popular Ba'al, represented by a bull, was served through bestiality (copulation with a bull).

8. One law for all. The pagan gods allowed noblemen to get off scot-free for crimes requiring severe punishments for others. Thus injustice was institutionalized. In contrast, biblical religion upheld the same standards for king and commoner alike. No one was above the law.

9. Persons more valuable than property. Whereas in Babylon—to cite just one example—property was more important than persons (as in the Code of Hammurabi), in Judaism it was the other way around. In the Ten Commandments and the rest of the Torah, the focus is on relationships: first God (commandments 1–4), and then others (commandments 5–10).

10. Women respected. For example, the radical fifth commandment doesn't read, "Honor your father," but "Honor your father and your mother." Inheritance law applied to daughters, not just sons. Divorce law provided for the woman's needs, and a certificate protected her against future claims by an ex-husband. Many other examples could be provided. In Christianity, of course, the place of women was elevated even further.

A religion that transcended culture

We've focused on ten ways in which the faith of the Jews was unique. Search for these truths in other ancient religions—and good luck trying! Anyone who thinks that Old Testament Judaism is just one more in a long litany of ancient religions has failed to do his homework! No ancient religion is like this!

Far from Old Testament Judaism being primitive or outdated, the opposite is true. The Old Testament presents the truths that became foundational not just for Western culture, but specifically for Christianity.

Time and again we are surprised by the wisdom, purity, and truth of the precepts of Judaism. It transcended its culture, setting the pace for right living. In the ancient world, no world religion even came close to equaling Judaism for its revolutionary and refreshing truths.

If the Jews were to be counter-cultural, how about you and me? Have we perhaps forgotten how utterly different the true God is to all man-made substitutes? Have we underestimated the revolutionary nature of God's righteous kingdom?

Spreading the word

The point of our study of religions is to gain a global perspective on world faiths, so that we may more deeply appreciate the true God, and better share him with others.

This will be our task in the next chapter. We'll boil down the basic similarities and differences among the religions, and offer a biblical strategy for interacting with people from other faiths.

CHAPTER 33
Answering Misconceptions About Religion

*O*ur modern world, especially in the industrialized regions, seems to have a love/hate relationship with religion. Being "spiritual" is cool; being religious is not. An old billboard reads, "Christ—yes; the church—no." People reject God and Christianity, yet consult astrologers or believe in reincarnation. And the intolerant insistence on "tolerance"—that everyone agree that all have an equal claim to truth (no one is really right or wrong)—is glaringly self-contradictory.

Even in Jesus' day, wrong thinking about religion and faith was common. That's why he challenged leaders and followers, the religious and the irreligious alike. Jesus asked many questions to make us think about faith. The Lord also was great at answering questions, and this book aims to equip us to emulate him.

In this chapter we suggest cogent answers to ten common misconceptions about religion—many of these misconceptions revisit information and objections we have covered throughout the book.

1. "Religion is only psychological projection. Humans created religion to assuage their fears, imaging spiritual powers and projecting their thinking onto a non-existent 'heavenly' canvas."
Although anthropologists note that some primitive peoples worship a single god, the Bible speaks of idolatry in the earliest historical phase of our species. Even if this is how religion initially appeared among humans, it doesn't mean that the objects of faith (God, the spiritual world, good, evil . . .) aren't real! Primitive worship would just be the process through which the Lord allowed our species to become aware of moral absolutes and the essential role of faith in every human's life.

2. "All religions are essentially the same."
The differences far outweigh the similarities. (Refer to chapter 31, "2500 Gods.")

3. "We made God in our image."
While this is true for religion generally speaking, it isn't true for Judaism and Christianity. God's central attribute is holiness. He is wholly other, wholly different from us. When we compare the "gods" of human religion to the God of the Bible, we realize just how surprising he is. Biblical faith isn't something anyone would invent; it rests upon revelation from God himself.

4. "We should be tolerant of others, not judging them."
True tolerance accepts people, even when we disagree with their ideas. Tolerance of ideas—the mistaken notion that all ideas have equal claim to be true—is a recent redefinition, forced upon Western society in the past century or so. (Refer to chapter 3, "Intolerance.")

5. "Religion is too confining. I want to be free, not under obligation."
There's no such thing as absolute freedom. Only God is fully free. We live every day of our lives under a number of restrictions, whether or not we are religious. All of us need to follow the laws of the land, take care of our health, observe social etiquette, earn (not steal) our money, and so on. The biblical truth may be even more surprising. We are all

slaves to sin and the flesh, or to righteousness and the Spirit (John 8:34; Rom 6:1–8:13).

6. "Religion is 'personal,' and should be kept that way."
Traditionally religion has been both private *and* public. And of course it's personal, because God is personal, and Christianity is all about relationships! It is *because* religion is personal that we want to share our faith with other persons. After all, the way of Christianity is a person (John 14:6).

7. "Sincerity is what counts."
We can be sincerely wrong, or sincerely right. In neither case does sincerity create truth—though it's a valuable quality for grasping the challenging truths of God's word.

8. "Christianity is the biggest killer."
Christ never authorized many of the acts that have been performed in his name. In fact, up until the Middle Ages, the church was universally pacifist.

9. "Religion poisons everything."
So claimed the late Christopher Hitchens in his bestseller *god is Not Great*. (Yes, *he decapitalized* God!) Organized religion, he claims is "violent, irrational, intolerant, allied to racism, tribalism, and bigotry, invested in ignorance and hostile to free inquiry, contemptuous of women and coercive toward children" (56). But what is going on here? Is religion doing the poisoning, or has religion been poisoned by the world? I found Hitchens' book easy to read and entertaining, but he offered little proof for his sweeping claim. For religious discussion to make any real headway, we have to separate personal bias (and animus) from the facts.

10. "Most of the world has already heard the gospel anyway, so there's no urgency."
Of course it depends on what you mean by "heard" and "gospel." Were they listening? And to which version of the gospel (Gal 1:6–9;

2 Cor 11:2–4)? At least in the 111 countries where I have traveled, people typically respond with surprise when I share the gospel with them. The information is new; the word has not usually been received through their temples, shrines, or even churches. No—it will not do to excuse ourselves with the belief that all the world has heard the word, or has access to the Bible. We need to go and tell them!

CHAPTER 34

Building Bridges, Not Burning Them

*J*t's time to summarize our findings about world religions. It's also time to think strategically: how can we best represent Christ as we continue to interact with followers of other world faiths?

Once you explore and compare the major faith traditions of the world, several general observations emerge:

1. All religions have *something* to say about life's basic existential questions (purpose, meaning, morality, ethics, identity, relationships, origin, destiny), yet it's the Bible that gives the most reasonable answers. My favorite analogy: moonlight (reflected) vs. sunlight (incandescent). The truth of God is reflected, if only dimly, in all religions. Yet for the truth itself (himself), we must come to the true God.

2. The differences between religions *greatly* outweigh the similarities. And the greatest difference? In his grace, the Almighty God bridges the gulf between man and God—personally. This happens through Christ's incarnation, crucifixion, resurrection, and the gift of the Spirit.

3. God is the just judge. He will unfairly condemn no one. While as Christians we believe Jesus' affirmation that he is the only way to the Father (John 14:6), we leave final judgment in God's hands.

4. We ought to respect all persons, regardless of religion—or lack of religion. We have something in common with everyone, but increasingly so with those who share more of our convictions about spiritual reality.

Increasing degrees of commonality

- We have something in common with every fellow human being. Made in God's likeness, he or she is a potential brother or sister. All humans are God's "children" (Acts 17:28), though they may not necessarily be sons or daughters in a right relationship with him (John 1:12–13). Please see graphic at douglasjacoby.com, search word Graphic 2.

- We have more in common with believers. We should always genuinely respect faith, since it entails humility, seeking, purity, and so on. Thus at some level we relate more to polytheists and even animists—for all acknowledge a spiritual reality—than we do to agnostics or atheists.

- We always have much more in common with our fellow monotheists. Their numbers are growing.

- Among the monotheists, we have a great deal in common with those in the Christian bloc, regardless of denomination. We may be keenly aware of what separates us (differing views on grace, free will, the Spirit, and so on). The watching world often struggles to grasp some distinctions we hold so sacred.

- Yet we have the most in common with true disciples (John 8:32, 13:34, 15:8) —those living under the lordship of Christ. We all agree on the standard of truth, and together are striving to live in a way that pleases the Lord.

Be informed; be respectful.

The Apostle Peter, writing to believers suffering amidst the diversity and worldliness of Greco-Roman paganism, offers invaluable guidance:

Who is going to harm you if you are eager to do good? But even if you should suffer for what is right, you are blessed. Do not fear their threats; do not be frightened. But in your hearts revere Christ as Lord. Always be prepared to give an answer to everyone who asks you to give the reason for the hope that you have. But do this with gentleness and respect, keeping a clear conscience. (1 Pet 3:13–16a).

- **The world isn't always friendly to faith.** In the face of hostility, we may give in to fear (see also 3:6). The context of the passage is opposition (also 4:12–16). Faced with mocking and persecution, Christians may be tempted to back off their commitment. The key to courage despite hostility and suffering is to remain conscious of Christ's presence (his power, example, and message).
- **We need to speak out of preparation.** When it comes to religion (like politics), there are a lot of opinions flying around. Some are based on facts. Most are simply a homespun blend of rumor and caricature. This is not the way the Lord wants us to speak about, or with, Muslims, Hindus, and others, especially when they're not part of the conversation or able to defend themselves.
- **Gentleness and respect are crucial.** Spiritual power doesn't consist in out-shouting one's opponent, or living a more "radical" life. The world is full of groups and individuals deeply committed to what they believe true. Spirituality, like leadership, requires the humility of Christ (Matt 5:3–9; 11:28–29). We must never resort to words or actions that violate our conscience. Whether engaged in dialogue, evangelism, teaching, preaching, or even everyday conversation, let's remain above reproach. The world is watching!

Share in the mission

Our God is completely able to draw all men to himself (John 6:44, 12:32)— not just lapsed Christians or exceptionally wide-open seekers. "All" includes every faith tradition—and even those with no faith tradition whatsoever. That is the only way Rev 7:9 will ever become a reality. The good news: Vast numbers of Hindus, Muslims, and Buddhists are being baptized into Christ. Jews, Sikhs, Jains, Mormons, and New Agers are coming to faith. Agnostics and atheists are turning to God. The Christian gospel is for everybody.

God works *through people* to reach people. If you want to be part of this exciting process, then confidence is a valuable asset. Not a confidence based on strong opinion or ego, but the confidence that comes when we revere Christ as Lord in our hearts. The confidence that comes when we have studied and prepared to converse with people from a variety of backgrounds and perspectives: Western faiths, Eastern religions, agnosticism, atheism, skepticism, and every place between. When we are prepared, we are no longer insecure or intimidated. As intimidation gives way to love, preparation and genuine respect pay off in meaningful conversations.

I hope this book has boosted your confidence, reminded you of the uniqueness of Christ, and emboldened you to stand firm in your faith. Let's join together in building bridges, since Christianity is a truly global faith.

About the Author

Douglas Jacoby is a frequent conference speaker, lecturing, teaching, and preaching in 120 nations. His specialty is Christian evidences. Douglas is a graduate of Duke University (history), Harvard Divinity School (New Testament), and Drew University (ministry). In addition, he is a university professor, debater, tour guide in the biblical world, and author of 30 books. He and his wife, Vicki, live in the Atlanta area.

His website has 10,000 pages and hundreds of podcasts. Visit **www.douglasjacoby.com**.

Notes

1 Kelly Shattuck, "7 Startling Facts: An Up Close Look at Church Attendance in America," *Church Leaders* website, accessed 12–14–2015, http://www.churchleaders.com/pastors/pastor-articles/139575-7-startling-facts-an-up-close-look-at-church-attendance-in-america.html.

2 Ed Stetzer, "Marriage, Divorce, and the Church: What do the Stats Say, and Can Marriage Be Happy?," *Christianity Today* online (February 14, 2014), accessed 12–14–2015: http://www.christianitytoday.com/edstetzer/2014/february/marriage-divorce-and-body-of-christ-what-do-stats-say-and-c.html.

3 Jeff Logue, "Pornography Statistics: Who Uses Porn?," *Thought Hub* website (October 22, 2015), accessed 12–14–2015: http://www.sagu.edu/thoughthub/pornography-statistics-who-uses-pornography.
   See also "Proven Men: Statistics on Pornography and Addiction," *Proven Men* website, accessed 12–14–2015: http://www.provenmen.org/2014pornsurvey/pornography-use-and-addiction/.

4 Michael Lindsay, quoted by Eric Gorski in "Many Paths to God," *South Bend Tribune* (June 24, 2008), A3.

5 For more information, see my article, "The Dead Sea Scrolls: 30 Questions and Answers," DouglasJacoby.com (July 17, 2003):

http://www.douglasjacoby.com/the-dead-sea-scrolls-30-questions-and-answers/.

6   For more on why the KJV-only argument unravels, listen to my podcast, "Is the KJV (the King James Version) the true Bible?," DouglasJacoby.com (May 25, 2015): http://www.douglasjacoby.com/kjv-king-james-version-true-bible/.

7   C.S. Lewis, *Mere Christianity* (New York, New York: HarperCollins, 1952).

8   This explanation is an adaptation from Plato, who wrote nearly four centuries before the birth of Christ. The original query concerned the Greek gods, who are bound by space and time, and often morally inferior to the mortals over whom they rule. The gods have little in common with the One we know through Christ.

9   D. A. Carson, *How Long, O Lord? Reflections on Suffering and Evil* (Downers Grove, Ill: InterVarsity Press, 1991), 44.

10 Friedrich Nietzsche, *Beyond Good and Evil*, IV.108 and IX.291.

11 For more on the nature of God, listen to my podcast, "The Gender of God," DouglasJacoby.com (February 3, 2014): http://www.douglasjacoby.com/godgendermp3/.

12 To study this topic further, I suggest my books *What's the Truth About Heaven and Hell?* (Harvest House, 2013) and *What Happens When We Die* (IPI, 2012).

13 Blaise Pascal, *The Pensées*, 7.430.

14 Paul Tillich wrote about this idea in *Dynamics of Faith* (Harper & Row, 1957).

15 I've engaged in several cordial debates with agnostic Michael Shermer. I've also debated atheists Richard Carrier, Robert Price, and Robert Brotherus.

16 Over a millennium earlier Augustine of Hippo (354-430 AD) had made the same point: "Some people read a book in order to discover God. But there is a greater book—the actual appearance of created things. Look above and below you, and note and read. The God that you wanted to discover did not write in letters of ink, but put in front of your eyes the very things that he made. Can you ask for a louder voice than that?" – *Sermons* 68.6

17 William Lane Craig, in The Lane-Craig Debate: Does God Exist?, with Douglas M. Jesseph, North Carolina State University, 1996. Transcript and notes available at http://www.leaderu.com/offices/ billcraig/docs/jesseph-craig2.html. Accessed 12–14–2015.

18 Henry M. Morris, *The Young Earth: The Real History of the Earth— Past, Present, and Future* (Green Forest, AR: Master Books, 1994), 4.

19 Henry M. Morris and John D. Morris, *The Modern Creation Trilogy* (Green Forest, AR: Master Books, 1996), 55.

20 Christopher Hitchens, *god Is Not Great: How Religion Poisons Everything* (New York: Twelve, 2007), 9.

21 Charles Darwin in a letter to John Fordyce, May 7, 1879.

22 Billy Graham, *Personal Thoughts by a Public Man* (Chariot Victor Pub, 1997).

23 For more on these various approaches, visit The American Scientific Affiliation's website, accessed 11–23–2015, http://www. asa3.org/ASA/education/origins/methods2.htm.

24 Augustine, *De Genesi ad Litteram*, I, xix, 39.

25 Erwin Schrödinger, *Nature and the Greeks* (Cambridge: Cambridge University Press, 1954).

26 Victor E. Frankl, *Man's Search for Meaning* (Boston: Beacon Press, 1959).

27 https://www.barna.org/research/faith-christianity/research-release/ perceptions-jesus-christians-evangelism-uk#.VsIIRBhnQiE.

28 For more information, check out my podcast, "Jesus: The Historical Evidence," DouglasJacoby.com (September 19, 2015): http://www.douglasjacoby.com/jesus-historical-evidence/.

29 For more on this, you might find my book *The Spirit* helpful (IPI, 2005).

30 To learn more about the fundamentals of Islam, you might want to read my book *Jesus & Islam* (IPI, 2009). For more, read some of the Qur'an, or listen to it being recited.

31 For a heart-moving talk on this very subject, please listen to my Palestinian friend Aziz Sarah share in a podcast about how he (as a Muslim) came to see Jews and Christians through fresh eyes: "The

Wolf Will Lie Down with the Lamb," DouglasJacoby.com (April 28, 2010): http://www.douglasjacoby.com/wolfmp3/.

32   While Christians don't conceive of God as a sexual being (masculine or feminine in the human sense), we do experience him as Father. When we say Jesus is Son of God, we don't mean that God had a wife, or that the Son of God came into existence when Mary conceived. Among the ancient Arabian tribes, the gods and goddesses had offspring. I am guessing that the popular Christianity of Muhammad's day, with its recently embraced devotion to Mary as Mother of God and obsession with prayers to the saints, felt to Muhammad more polytheistic than monotheistic. All historical considerations aside, Father is definitely not one of Allah's 99 names. Think about that.

33   Perhaps if we who are Christians would see the Muslims as Jesus sees them, we'd have more of an impact. Instead of hiding from Muslims, skulking around afraid to share our faith, we could be known as God's sincere, giving, and joyous people. We would invite Muslims to dinner, stand up for them when they are misrepresented, and even appreciate the truths their religion proclaims. Instead of setting ourselves up to be labeled as "infidels" and "hypocrites" (as is too often the case), we would be perceived by our Muslim neighbors as knowledgeable about our Scriptures and theirs, eager to build bridges, and respectful (though never compromising).

34   Kelly Shattuck, "7 Startling Facts: An Up Close Look at Church Attendance in America," *Church Leaders* website, accessed 12–14–2015, http://www.churchleaders.com/pastors/pastor-articles/139575-7-startling-facts-an-up-close-look-at-church-attendance-in-america.html.

35   In the East, it is thought that we err when we fail to realize our divinity. The "secret," according to Australia's Rhonda Byrne, author of *The Secret*: "I am god!" Another consequence of subjective truth is that all religions are relativized. Thus in the popular film *The Life of Pi* (based on Yann Martel's novel of the same name), Piscine "Pi" Molitor is brought up Hindu, comes to God through Christ, and learns to worship through Islam.

Morgan James
Speakers Group

We connect Morgan James published
authors with live and online events
and audiences who will benefit
from their expertise.

Morgan James makes all of our titles available
through the Library for All Charity Organizations.

www.LibraryForAll.org

Printed in the USA
CPSIA information can be obtained
at www.ICGtesting.com
JSHW022341140824
68134JS00019B/1626

9 781683 500285